DO YOU KNOW EVERYTHING ABOUT THE 7TH ART?

Wordsearch

HISTORY of CINEMA
1895 - 2023

The Ultimate Word Search Book on the History of Cinema

WORDWEABER PUBLISHING
A PLACE ONLY FOR THE WORDSEARCH LOVERS

WORDWEABER PUBLISHING
A PLACE ONLY FOR THE WORDSEARCH LOVERS

No part of this book may be scanned, reproduced or distributed in any printed or electronic form without the prior permission of the author or publisher.

COPYRIGHT 2024 - WORDWEABER PUBLISHING

★★★★★

We love to receive reviews from our customers. If you had the opportunity to provide a review we would greatly appreciate it.
Thank you!

¡Welcome to the History of Cinema like you've never been told before!

Get ready for an unprecedented cinematic adventure with this word search book! It's not just any book; it's a portal to the rich history of cinema, filled with dazzling illustrations, fascinating anecdotes, and curiosities that will ignite your love for movies with a new passion. From the initial hesitations of silent film to the dazzling digital era, this book takes you by the hand on an exciting journey through the most emblematic moments of the seventh art.

Imagine unraveling the secrets of word searches while discovering behind-the-scenes stories that will surprise you, make you laugh, and maybe even cry. Each page is a window to a different era, each illustration a door to a forgotten world, each anecdote a spark that illuminates the shadows of film history.

This book is a multifaceted gem for anyone who cherishes cinema. It offers an opportunity to delve into the craftsmanship, history, and evolution of film while uncovering hidden gems and gaining insights into the lesser-spoken aspects of the movie world. Whether you're solving puzzles, immersing yourself in the illustrations, or savoring the anecdotes and facts, this book promises a comprehensive, entertaining, and educational experience that celebrates cinema's legacy in our lives.

So, whether you're a die-hard cinephile or just someone looking for a new way to connect with cinema, this book promises to be your perfect companion. It invites you to explore, to learn, and above all, to celebrate cinema in all its forms. Welcome to a spectacular journey through the History of Cinema, where each word search is an adventure and every word a revelation!

CONTENT
CHAPTER ONE

TO PLAY

Early Cinema Days - p.9
Silent Film Stars - p.11
Silent Film Innovations - p.12
Silent Film Pionners - p.13
Transition to Sound - p.15
Pioneering Women in Early Cinema - p.17
1930s Adventure & Action - p.19
1930s Golden Age Begins - p.21
1930s Genres - p.22
1930s Actresses - p.24
1930s Actors - p.26
1930s Film Innovations - p.27
War Time Cinema - p.29
International Film of the Era - p.30
Key Films of the Golden Age - p.32
Industry Changes - p.34
Early Animation & Cartoons - p.36
Great Film Directors of the 1930s - p.38
Iconic 1930s Film Characters - p.39
Breakthroughs in Film Sound & Music - p.41
The Impact of The Great Depression on Cinema - p.43
Major Film Studios of the Golden Age - p.44
Notable Film Critics & Theorist - p.46
Advances in Film Technology - p.47
Landmark Films of the Era - p.48

TO KNOW

Lumiere Brothers. The Fathers of Cinema - p.8
Silent Film Stars - p.10
The Jazz Singer. The First Sound Film - p.14
Pioneering Women - p.16
King-Kong - p.18
Did you know?... (Lion MGM) - P.20
The Goddesses of The Golden Age - p.23
Did you know... (Clark Gable) - p.25
War Time Cinema - p.28
Metropolis - p.31
The First Oscars Ceremony - p.33
Early Animation & Cartoons - p.35
John Ford. The Portraitist of the Human Condition - p.37
Did you know?... (The Wizard of Oz) - p.40
The Great Depression - p.42
Did you know that Truffaut was a critic? - p.45

CHAPTER TWO

TO PLAY

Hollywood During Wotld War II - p.51
Post-War Cinema - p.52
Golden Age Film Stars - p.54
1950s & 1960s Directors - p.56
Iconic Films of the 1950s - p.58
Rise of Tlevision - p.59
New Wave Movements - p.60
Sci-Fi & Fantasy of the 1960s - p.61
Music & Concert Films - p.63
Social Revolution in Cinema - p.65
Cinema in the Cold War - p.66
Major Film Genres of the 1970s & 1980s - p.68
Blockbuster Era Begins - p.70
New Hollywood Directors - p.72
Iconic Actors & Actresses of the 70s & 80s - p.74
Influential International Cinema - p.76
1980s Teen & Family Films - p.78
Advances in Film Technology - p.80
Cult Film & Movements - p.82
Documentary & Realism - p.83
Rise of Action Heroes & Superheroes - p.85
Landmark Science Fiction Films - p.87
Comedy Icons of the 70s & 80s - p.89
Influential Female Directors - p.91
Breakthrough in Animation & Special Effects - p.93

TO KNOW

Hollywood During World War II - p.50
James Dean. An Eternal Icon - p.53
Orson "Citizen" Welles - p.55
Seven Samurai - p.57
Music & Cinema - p.62
Social Revolution in Cinema - p.64
The Godfather - p.67
Rocky Balboa - p.69
Stanley Kubrick - p.71
Meryl Streep - p.73
The Master Buñuel. Survivor & Genius - p.75
Back to the Future. An Iconic Legacy Through Time - p.77
When Monsters & Creatures Came to Life - p.79
The Indie Movement - p.81
Superman (1978) - p.84
Did you know?... (Science Fiction Films) - p.86
Bill Murray - p.88
Kathryn Bigelow - p.90
Breakthrough in Animation & Special Effects - p.92

CHAPTER THREE

TO PLAY

Cinema in the 1990s - p.96
Influential Films of the 1990s - p.98
Rise of Animation Studios - p.100
Major Film Genres of the 90s & 2000s - p.101
2000s New Wave & Indie Directors - p.103
Global Cinema in the New Millennium - p.105
Influential 2000s Films - p.107
Modern Animation & CGI Advances - p.109
Documentary Films & Realism - p.111
Rise of Streaming Services - p.112
21st Century Film Technology - p.113
New Genres & Trends - p.114
Influential Women in Modern Cinema - p.116
Modern Science Fiction & Fantasy - p.117
Independent Cinema Evolution - p.119
Global Box Office Hits - p.121
Trends in 21st Century Storytelling - p.122
Modern Film Soundtracks & Scores - p.124
Changing Landscapes of Film Distribution - p125
Social Impact Films - p.127
Evolution of Superhero Movies - p.129
Social Media & Cinema - p. 131
Iconic Film Characters of the 21st Century - p.133
Revolutionary Directors of the 2000s - p.135

TO KNOW

Quentin Tarantino. The Rebel of Modern Cinema - p.95
Forrest Gump. Heart, Comedy & History - p.97
Pixar Animation Studios - p.99
Wes Anderson. A Parallel Universe - p.102
Bollywood. Bringing Cultures Together Through Dance - p.104
Amelie. A love Letter to Parisian Magic - p.106
Shrek. An Ogre & a Donkey That Enchanted the World - p.108
Document to Transform - p.110
Influential Women in Modern Cinema - p.115
Independent Cinema Evolution - p.118
Avatar. James Cameron's Life Project - p.120
Modern Film Soundtracks & Scores - p.123
Milk. Inspiration & Activism - p.126
Superhero Tsunami - p.128
The Impact of the Digital Age on the Industry - p.130
The JOKER of Joaquin Phoenix - p.132
Christopher Nolan - p.134

SOLUTIONS - p.137 / p.155

CHAPTER ONE
1895-1940

Lumiere Brothers. The Fathers of Cinema

The Lumière brothers, Auguste and Louis, are key figures in the history of cinema, recognized as pioneers in the development of cinematic technology. Hailing from France, these innovative siblings combined their technical ingenuity and passion for photography to create the Lumière Cinématographe, a revolutionary device capable of capturing, developing, and projecting moving images.

In the 1890s, working in their father's photographic factory in Lyon, the Lumière brothers embarked on the challenge of improving and expanding the possibilities of moving images, which at that time were limited by devices such as Thomas Edison's Kinetoscope, which allowed the viewing of moving images by a single person through a viewer.

The Lumière's innovation came with the creation of the Cinématographe in 1895. This device was notably lighter and more versatile than existing devices and had the unique ability to record, copy, and project images. Their first film, "La Sortie de l'Usine Lumière à Lyon" (Workers Leaving the Lumière Factory in Lyon), simply captured the employees leaving the Lumière factory and is considered one of the first films in history.

On December 28, 1895, the Lumière brothers organized the first public commercial film screening in the Salon Indien du Grand Café on the Boulevard des Capucines in Paris. This historic screening included ten short films, each lasting about 50 seconds. The event marked the birth of cinema as a form of collective entertainment and transformed the way stories could be told and experienced, inaugurating a new era in art and communication.

Despite their initial success, the Lumière brothers did not see a long-term future in cinema, considering it a mere curiosity without much commercial or artistic potential. They focused on other inventions and technical contributions. However, their legacy endures, and they are celebrated as the fathers of cinema, having paved the way for the development of this powerful form of art and entertainment.

Early Cinema Days
1895 - 1940

A	G	G	Z	T	T	I	W	Z	E	Y	W	H	A	K	R	Q	C
R	W	H	E	C	V	Q	A	N	G	D	U	R	V	T	Z	W	D
W	N	Y	M	E	L	I	E	S	D	U	M	C	F	R	X	P	M
U	C	W	G	P	Q	E	P	X	A	O	N	Z	U	N	W	D	F
Z	U	G	Z	R	A	F	Y	W	W	I	O	W	J	A	B	U	X
G	W	M	C	D	S	N	T	S	A	S	E	T	B	I	Q	K	W
F	Q	I	V	I	Y	K	O	A	M	X	D	O	Q	W	A	T	B
H	Y	L	W	C	I	N	E	M	A	T	O	G	R	A	P	H	V
E	Y	Q	V	F	F	O	R	P	X	K	L	L	C	M	X	E	A
R	B	R	Q	O	S	J	R	O	J	L	E	Z	T	F	F	U	A
E	P	O	C	S	O	T	E	N	I	K	K	I	R	I	X	T	H
I	L	B	O	Q	E	I	U	Z	R	D	C	P	L	S	Z	G	W
M	E	U	S	J	Q	O	G	W	A	N	I	M	A	T	I	O	N
U	J	G	Q	B	Q	U	A	Z	Z	T	N	G	E	H	G	A	J
L	T	P	R	Z	K	I	D	U	P	J	O	K	V	J	D	J	C
Y	Q	C	Y	Q	O	T	D	V	F	K	G	B	X	M	Z	F	R
C	B	I	F	B	Y	Z	R	Z	N	D	S	B	I	M	L	J	N
H	P	R	O	J	E	C	T	O	R	D	E	D	I	S	O	N	U

SOLUTION ON PAGE 137

CINEMATOGRAPH **NICKELODEON** **EDISON** **MELIES** **ANIMATION**
DAGUERREOTYPE **KINETOSCOPE** **LUMIERE** **FILM** **PROJECTOR**

Charles Chaplin and Jackie Coogan in the iconic frame from the movie "The Kid" Dir. by Charles Chaplin (1921)

Silent Film Stars

The arrival of Silent Cinema marks the beginning of the film industry and an era of innovation in visual storytelling. In the late 19th century, inventors and pioneers like the Lumière brothers in France and Thomas Edison in the United States developed the first devices capable of capturing and projecting sequences of moving images, bringing to life what would eventually be known as cinema.

Silent cinema, which predominated from the late 1890s to the late 1920s, was characterized by films without synchronized sound, where the story was primarily told through facial expressions, body gestures, and intertitles that provided dialogue and narration. This era saw the rise of the first film stars, such as Charlie Chaplin, Buster Keaton, and Mary Pickford, whose performances transcended language barriers and earned them fans worldwide.

Silent film screenings were often accompanied by live music, varying from a solitary pianist to a full orchestra, depending on the venue, to enhance the emotional and narrative experience of the films. Genres such as slapstick comedy, drama, and romance flourished during this era, establishing the foundations of cinematic language and genre conventions that would continue to evolve over time.

The silent cinema era came to an end with the advent of sound cinema in the late 1920s, marking the beginning of a new chapter in film history. However, the narrative and stylistic techniques developed during the silent period have had a lasting impact on the art of cinema, influencing generations of filmmakers and continuing to fascinate audiences today.

Silent Film Stars
1900 - 1920

G	K	U	Z	M	O	X	B	D	G	S	U	X	Z
O	N	I	T	N	E	L	A	V	M	N	D	Z	Y
L	O	Y	T	E	O	B	R	A	G	K	W	G	V
E	S	R	B	Z	Z	F	R	L	H	I	H	F	A
V	N	Y	U	N	Z	C	Y	L	A	M	I	S	S
E	A	U	L	T	O	Q	M	C	R	I	W	K	G
V	W	X	M	S	J	Y	O	S	B	D	U	N	D
F	S	K	H	F	Y	R	R	H	U	U	U	A	Z
B	V	N	I	E	L	S	E	N	C	H	C	B	K
M	I	S	O	V	E	P	I	C	K	F	O	R	D
H	C	S	C	T	C	H	A	P	L	I	N	I	C
L	S	B	M	Q	A	N	E	I	E	H	L	A	I
B	W	E	W	I	U	E	E	E	L	P	E	F	A
R	A	O	U	K	P	Z	K	M	J	Q	H	T	X

SOLUTION ON PAGE 137

| VALENTINO | ARBUCKLE | NIELSEN | PICKFORD | KEATON |
| FAIRBANKS | BARRYMORE | CHAPLIN | SWANSON | GARBO |

Silent Film Innovations

```
E P E S G Y I W M L O J J C Z
V L X G M Q E P X R H Q X L H
O Z T N A A T D K T C W R R F
M I H I F T D V F Q L B B T R
K Z Y T T I N A S C R L E R S
D R D H R R B O J L U G U V S
X O K G T O E U M N L C X P T
E F L I T Z F T O F W U D I R
H L F L X Y F E N Y E N A R C
C W M C Y W E A J I F R X B E
G O N C I F C L O S E U P L C
Q M F B M T N A M O W W C P
W R D P F A S E A N W S T M Z
J E Y J K E G C X P H T N U I
P T Q G N I T N I T H O H B E
```

SOLUTION ON PAGE 137

INTERTITLE CAMERA DOLLY EFFECTS TINTING
LIGHTING   CLOSEUP PAN   MONTAGE CRANE

12

Silent Film Pionners

```
Z Y M W I D T R K S X R D O P
G C M X U Y J E T A G R K J I
Y O I W Z A W I V Y R E W F P
O T E I S E N S T E I N O S H
P G H A H S U R I W F O J G M
R Z O T B F E H U S F I M G Z
G H R L D H D N X M I R I U S
F D T Y A P R Z N Q T S S F B
U C S L P N Z Z S E H Q L L V
J X F B I I G T Y F T W M V U
G V L H V X S T M V O T R E V
O W C V B G D V V Q T P B L A
P O P B X M S P E J P M D U G
E Z A B O A D T D U W O G M I
T A F Z X H M S L K Q B J V B
```

SOLUTION ON PAGE 137

EISENSTEIN **FLAHERTY** **LANG** **SENNETT** **GRIFFITH**
STROHEIM **MURNAU** **GISH** **RENOIR** **VERTOV**

May McAvoy and Al Jolson in a frame from "The Jazz Singer" Dir.by Alan Crosland (1927)

The Jazz Singer. The first sound film

"The Jazz Singer" is considered the first full-length sound film and marked a milestone in the history of cinema. Released in 1927, this film directed by Alan Crosland and starring Al Jolson, is known for being the first to feature synchronized spoken dialogue, thanks to the Vitaphone system, which combined image projection with phonographic discs for audio.

The plot revolves around Jakie Rabinowitz, played by Jolson, a young Jewish man who defies his family's traditions by pursuing a career in jazz instead of following in his father's footsteps as a cantor in the synagogue. The film is famous for the scene where Jolson says, "Wait a minute, wait a minute, you ain't heard nothin' yet," moments before breaking into song, thus marking the transition from silent to sound cinema.

Although "The Jazz Singer" primarily contains music and sound effects, and its spoken dialogue is limited, its success demonstrated the enormous potential of sound cinema, initiating Hollywood's transition to "talking" movies. The film was not only a commercial success but also had a significant cultural impact, heralding the end of the silent film era.

"The Jazz Singer" is also remembered for its jazz elements and Al Jolson's performance in "blackface," a practice that is controversial today but was common in theater and cinema at the time. The film is an important document of its era, reflecting both technological advancements in the film industry and the cultural and racial tensions of the time.

Transition to Sound
1927

```
R U K D M B I Z H K R H B I V
U S E I M I U T Y E R O C S N
G K V A Z Q C W M N V O F R T
U D N L O O P R P O K I L A U
Q Z O O K Z R I O H E K A A K
T H R G F M V V K P K L M G F
H E C U R V R Q T A H P W P G
W Y W E M X E V W T L O L U H
H M T F K I N F E I I J N A A
B X Z U O Y T M F V G M J E P
P P Z U Q L Q I A E I X D V G
K T A L K I E S Y N C M T L G
E T J S E R I Y Y K K T C G Y
U M Y V S U L X L K K D S Q V
J S M Z Q X G U B P K S O A J
```

SOLUTION ON PAGE 138

| MICROPHONE | VITAPHONE | SYNC | AMPLIFIER | SCORE |
| DIALOGUE | EFFECTS | JAZZ | TALKIES | FOLEY |

Mary Pickford, Marlene Dietrich and Barbara Stanwyck

Pioneering Women

In the nascent film industry of the early 20th century, a group of extraordinary women emerged as pioneers, leaving an indelible mark with their talent, resilience, and star power. Mary Pickford, the "America's Sweetheart," wasn't just adored for her charm and acting prowess; she was also a shrewd businesswoman and a co-founder of United Artists, setting a precedent for artists' control over their careers and creations.

Clara Bow, the "It Girl," became the embodiment of the free-spirited and vivacious Jazz Age. Her on-screen presence defined the image of the modern flapper and helped Hollywood capture the imagination of a generation eager to break free from convention.

Lillian Gish, often called the "First Lady of Silent Cinema," elevated film acting to new artistic heights with her expressive performances. Her collaborations with D.W. Griffith helped to develop cinema's narrative language.

Myrna Loy, with her sophistication and poise, became the epitome of the modern woman on screen. Her "The Thin Man" series catapulted her to stardom, showcasing an on-screen chemistry and wit rarely seen before.

Marlene Dietrich and Greta Garbo brought an air of mystery and cosmopolitan sophistication to Hollywood. Dietrich, known for challenging gender norms, and Garbo, the enigmatic Swedish star, delivered performances that transcended language and culture, becoming global icons.

Mae West, meanwhile, was a force to be reckoned with for her bold sexuality and double entendre-laden dialogue. She pushed the boundaries of censorship and societal norms, becoming a voice for women's liberation.

Barbara Stanwyck, known for her versatility and strength, delivered performances that shattered the mold of what an actress could portray on screen, from comedies to intense dramas and film noir.

Jean Harlow, the "Platinum Blonde," became one of Hollywood's first sex symbols, and her bold style and personality made her a role model for actresses seeking to control their image and career.

Norma Shearer, one of the first actresses to challenge traditional roles for women on and off the screen, displayed a range and depth in her performances that defied the expectations of her era.

These women were more than actresses; they were innovators and entrepreneurs who shaped the film industry. Their legacy continues to be a source of inspiration and admiration, proving that talent and determination can break barriers and change the world.

Pioneering Women in Early Cinema

```
V Q I S W U X Z P F S S D
V Z Y Q F S D W G P Z P N
J X G B R Y W F F I I A R
X I E Y U O I O L C S G I
Y C U Y U W B B K B T H D
Z O E I S R D F Q S A S E
W O L R A H O L E A N M S
S M Q G S R E W B O W B N
E P Q B D S Y A R W Y A M
G V L R D I E T R I C H S
D Z B N W J X O R E K C O
T B I H T J V E Z R R G Y
Z Q E P F S Q D X H Z P G
```

SOLUTION ON PAGE 138

| STANWYCK | PICKFORD | GISH | WEST | DIETRICH |
| SHEARER | HARLOW | LOY | BOW | GARBO |

17

KING KONG

"King Kong" is a 1933 American film directed by Merian C. Cooper and Ernest B. Schoedsack. This adventure and monster movie classic tells the story of a giant prehistoric gorilla named Kong, who is captured on a remote island and brought to New York City for exhibition. The film is notable for its innovative special effects, including stop-motion animation, miniatures, and camera tricks, which at the time set new standards for special effects cinema.

The plot follows Carl Denham, a daring filmmaker who takes his team, including the beautiful actress Ann Darrow, played by Fay Wray, to the mysterious Skull Island in search of a living legend. There, they find Kong, who falls in love with Ann, leading to tragic and memorable events, including the iconic scene of Kong scaling the Empire State Building.

"King Kong" was not only a box office success but also received critical acclaim for its artistic and technical ambition. The film has been interpreted in various ways, from a critique of colonialism and exploitation to a tragedy about beauty and the beast. Over the years, "King Kong" has established itself as a cinematic masterpiece and has influenced countless monster and adventure films, making Kong one of the most recognizable icons in popular culture.

1930s Adventure & Action

```
I U K R W H G N Z E C B H J J N G
W E S T E R N D P U D O X D P X G
I G S U V L T D S G G P Z P G L F
D L N O U B K T J O E V G D B V M
Y F Z O R R O C U R B P O Y A T Q
B A C V K H E G U E I V B J R I X
A I U U A F C T P B O Y N U I E V
T R M O L K N Z S R H Z H O R M H
P B S Y T E X Y L G I S Z H S V T
J A N T V T L D O N N W A A S P N
W N Y D A A G O G Q I A Y W W F C
C K A B B R C N J V D I G C S D A
R S J U Q I Z B R S L R O G E E E
I S O Q E P B A G U R E S W F C F
Y S U V L X V Q N T E O F E E C E
C S Z D P I J N B N A J M F K H K
X I D D D T W F P E L Q C K U W O
```

SOLUTION ON PAGE 138

SWASHBUCKLER   ADVENTURE   WESTERN   GANGSTER   TARZAN
FAIRBANKS   PIRATE   ZORRO   FLYNN   KONG

Did you know?...

The creation of the iconic Metro-Goldwyn-Mayer (MGM) lion logo, known as "Leo the Lion," is an interesting part of cinema history. The first lion used for the logo was Slats, and his roar was not recorded; instead, titles appeared with him roaring silently from 1924 to 1928, during the silent film era. Slats was the only MGM lion that didn't roar, as his image was used during a period when films still had no sound.

The first time a roaring lion was recorded for the MGM logo was with his successor, Jackie, in 1928. This was the first "roaring" version of the logo and coincided with the arrival of sound cinema. Jackie was filmed roaring (although some reports suggest that the sound initially used was from a phonograph and not Jackie's actual roar) and this sound logo premiered with the movie "White Shadows in the South Seas." The roar became an iconic part of the logo and has been updated with different lions over the years.

The process of recording these lions for the logo involved filming the animal on a set that recreated an art environment with classic details. The lions were trained and handled by specialized caretakers to ensure their well-being during the filming process. Over the years, MGM has used several lions for its logo, each bringing its own unique presence to the iconic emblem.

The current lion, named Leo, has been MGM's mascot since 1957. Since then, the logo has not undergone any modifications.

1930s Golden Age Begins

N	J	U	S	Y	A	O	Z	D	Y	N	B	W	G
K	Q	T	S	C	R	Y	N	R	T	T	L	U	X
G	Z	R	N	M	O	O	R	A	I	X	F	B	B
Q	M	G	C	U	W	M	M	M	E	O	W	U	O
S	A	V	X	S	O	B	E	A	J	F	N	L	P
W	K	X	X	I	Y	M	V	D	N	N	C	I	M
F	B	D	O	C	L	M	A	V	I	C	X	V	Q
Y	M	J	K	A	L	J	M	R	V	A	E	K	Y
V	I	V	F	L	J	T	E	K	A	A	C	T	V
S	E	L	T	J	W	N	T	Y	J	P	A	Q	I
S	X	A	P	X	R	S	R	A	D	I	O	X	Y
M	M	L	H	A	L	R	O	A	R	B	N	N	U
Q	E	T	W	M	Z	V	P	G	T	I	P	B	K
Y	Z	C	F	Z	E	F	H	Y	C	U	V	N	K

SOLUTION ON PAGE 138

PARAMOUNT   METRO   COMEDIA   RADIO   ROMANCE
WARNER   FOX   DRAMA   NOIR   MUSICAL

1930s Genres

F	T	N	R	U	K	U	U	Z	Y	V	G	Y	T	U
E	U	V	E	R	S	Z	Z	L	W	B	G	Y	E	G
P	D	C	V	U	Q	C	G	K	C	V	S	J	C	G
V	M	H	I	S	T	O	R	I	C	A	L	U	N	Q
H	X	Q	T	P	D	C	Y	E	T	L	O	A	A	V
W	B	M	C	R	O	B	H	N	W	R	D	Q	M	S
F	K	W	E	D	O	I	A	B	I	B	F	R	O	K
Q	T	K	T	L	H	F	B	V	P	R	A	Y	R	S
Y	U	H	E	S	O	X	J	W	F	A	A	L	V	C
M	U	T	D	K	H	D	P	M	H	W	L	W	L	K
L	K	O	K	Y	V	P	R	A	F	F	I	G	T	M
J	R	O	R	R	O	H	G	A	N	G	S	T	E	R
S	C	C	Q	R	H	G	C	N	M	R	Q	K	Z	T
S	V	V	P	M	J	S	M	X	Y	A	E	P	U	E
N	D	X	L	H	F	E	O	W	T	I	O	G	X	D

SOLUTION ON PAGE 139

MELODRAMA	**HISTORICAL**	**DETECTIVE**	**ROMANCE**	**SCREWBALL**
FANTASY	**GANGSTER**	**HORROR**	**BIOPIC**	**WAR**

Katharine Hepburn

The Goddesses of the Golden Age

The Golden Age of Hollywood, particularly the 1930s, stands as a transformative era that shaped the film industry as we know it today. During this period, actresses were not only pivotal in film narratives but also emerged as cultural icons, setting trends, defining fashions, and often embodying societal ideals and challenges of their time.

Actresses of this era, such as Katharine Hepburn, Bette Davis, Joan Crawford, Greta Garbo, and Marlene Dietrich, were celebrated not just for their undeniable acting prowess but also for their ability to break conventional molds and challenge prevailing gender stereotypes. Katharine Hepburn, for instance, was known for her independent spirit and refusal to conform to the expected norms for women of her era, both on and off the screen. Bette Davis, on the other hand, earned a reputation for portraying complex, emotionally intense characters, paving the way for more nuanced and multidimensional roles for women in cinema.

The Golden Age also witnessed the solidification of the star system, where actresses were valued not only for their on-screen work but also for their public image, becoming true figures of influence. Their style, mannerisms, and conduct were emulated and admired by millions, establishing a new kind of relationship between celebrities and their audience.

Moreover, these actresses brought to the screen stories that delved into the complexities of the human condition, love, ambition, and the defiance of social conventions, contributing to a broader cultural dialogue that transcended the confines of cinema. In an era marked by significant social and economic changes, including the Great Depression, films offered not just an escape but also a reflection of society's dreams, fears, and aspirations.

The influence of these actresses extends beyond their time; their legacy continues to inspire generations of actors, filmmakers, and viewers. They represent not just the golden age of cinema but also a moment when cinematic art began to actively question and shape societal values and norms, establishing film's role as both a mirror and a shaper of popular culture.

In summary, the actresses of Hollywood's Golden Age were instrumental in the evolution of cinema, not just as entertainment but as a potent force in society, marking an unforgettable chapter in the history of cinematic art.

1930s Actresses

```
E K Q K H E P B U R N V L
O S G I M G T G S S J G F
S G R N K R I G U Z I J N
T I C E O C V E X A E Q X
J B V R G Q Y P L F H O U
K A E A A O D W O G C Z W
U Z Y K D W R Z N D I C F
E L I B H F F H N A R W E
O R D R A B M O L T T K S
Q C H C R P B V R D E S T
F W B Y L K R Q A D I F S
D B U Y O L A S N W D T P
J M K P W O R N V R M Z G
```

SOLUTION ON PAGE 139

| CRAWFORD | LOMBARD | DIETRICH | STANWYCK | DAVIS |
| HEPBURN | HARLOW | ROGERS | LEIGH | LOY |

24

Clark Gable

Did you know?...

Clark Gable was mistakenly registered as a girl at birth. Imagine the surprise! This curious fact marked the beginning of a life full of unexpected twists for the future "King of Hollywood".

Gable battled dyslexia. Despite struggling with dyslexia, Gable became one of the most beloved and respected actors of his time, proving that obstacles can be overcome with determination and talent.

His aversion to vests caused a fashion change. After appearing without a vest in a scene, vest sales dropped by 40%! Gable not only set trends on screen but also in men's attire.

Gable and the staircase in "Gone with the Wind". The famous scene where he carries Scarlett O'Hara up the stairs was a true test of endurance. After several exhausting takes, director Victor Fleming joked that he didn't need the last take, but wanted to see if Gable could do it one more time!

The nickname "The King". He earned this title after an incident with Spencer Tracy at MGM studios when Tracy, finding a crowd blocking Gable's car, exclaimed: "Long live the King!" This moment, followed by a joke where Tracy crowned Gable in an improvised ceremony, cemented his nickname, amplified by commentator Ed Sullivan.

His prank on the set of "Gone with the Wind". Gable played a prank on Hattie McDaniel (Mammy) by substituting her tea with whisky during the toast scene for Bonnie's birth. That prankster spirit definitely added a bit of sparkle behind the scenes!

The Nazi enemy who admired him. During World War II, Hermann Goering, Hitler's collaborator, allegedly put a price on Gable's head, not to eliminate him but to present him to Hitler, who was a great admirer of the actor!

Gable's dissatisfaction with Rhett Butler. Even though this role is one of the most iconic of his career, Gable was not pleased with the character of Rhett Butler, adding an intriguing layer to his legendary performance.

The legacy of his last work and his departure. "The Misfits" was Gable's last film, co-starring Marilyn Monroe. His death shortly after filming ended the chapter of an exceptionally lived life, leaving behind a legacy that still resonates in the film industry and popular culture.

1930s Actors

D	G	G	R	K	F	M	S	D	T	D	X
Z	A	A	A	P	I	F	C	Y	R	F	B
E	B	S	B	F	F	O	L	R	A	K	G
R	L	T	C	P	N	O	Y	H	W	C	D
F	E	A	D	N	O	F	E	A	E	H	B
Y	T	I	G	B	C	H	N	V	T	W	R
I	L	R	V	X	U	T	G	R	S	F	G
D	C	E	B	I	S	B	A	Y	H	L	M
Z	Z	A	A	O	L	G	C	W	W	S	S
L	Q	R	E	P	O	O	C	C	O	J	N
D	B	C	O	B	L	T	L	N	A	K	Z
V	P	C	K	V	Y	G	R	A	N	T	T

SOLUTION ON PAGE 139

STEWART   BOGART   COOPER   KARLOFF   ASTAIRE
CAGNEY   GABLE   GRANT   FONDA   OLIVIER

1930s Film Innovations

```
Y I A I H X O T H C P J Q F Z M
D Q Y T H P R D Q O R E W C Q K
X V I D E Q I S Z L O M V C S L
N M Q N F C M H I D T K J H O N
N P H U V Z H A S A U R X R U K
J E S U G G R N C R W D G O N C
E V W R Q I P Q I H O D I M D H
F P G S U B B P I C X S A A T B
G E G P R R R V U W O E N K R Z
S J F S L E I M G C F L V E A X
U L E Y C G E H J I L V O Y C T
K Q F O S N L L Q X O C Z R K C
D E D I T I N G C K D O P V B A
Y E S A N I M A T I O N K Q R C
C H R D C H V S P M D T Z O C S
M Y F S M Y S D F L Y T L C N O
```

SOLUTION ON PAGE 139

SOUNDTRACK   TECHNICOLOR   DOCUMENTARY   CHROMAKEY   NEWSREEL
ANIMATION   CENSORSHIP   PRECODE   EDITING   ZOOM

27

Still frame from the film "Casablanca" (1942), Dir. by Michael Curtiz

War-Time Cinema

During the late 1930s, specifically in the era leading up to and during World War II, the Hollywood film industry experienced significant changes and challenges. The advent of sound in cinema had already revolutionized the industry in the late 1920s, with films like "The Jazz Singer" in 1927 marking the transition to "talkies" and bringing audiences back to theaters in large numbers. This period saw the introduction of Technicolor, adding vibrant color to films, enhancing their appeal. However, the initial high costs and technical challenges meant that color films were not predominant until later.

The late 1930s to early 1940s, often referred to as the "Golden Age" of cinema, was a time of significant creativity and output in Hollywood. Despite the Great Depression's impact on the economy, the film industry thrived due to the escapism movies provided. Iconic films like "Gone With the Wind" and "The Wizard of Oz," both from 1939, showcased the advancements in color filmmaking and storytelling.

The onset of World War II brought Hollywood into close cooperation with the U.S. government, producing films that supported the war effort by boosting morale and propagating the "American way of life." These films ranged from straightforward patriotic themes to more nuanced stories that delved into the psychological and social challenges of the times. Directors such as Frank Capra and John Ford created documentaries and feature films that were meant to inform and support the troops and the public about the war's realities.

However, this period wasn't without its challenges. Post-war, the industry faced economic difficulties due to inflation, labor unrest, and the loss of foreign markets due to protectionist policies. The introduction of television in the 1940s also presented a significant challenge, offering free entertainment at home and reducing cinema attendance. In response, Hollywood began to focus on aspects that differentiated cinema from television, such as color films and widescreen formats, to draw audiences back.

The era also saw the rise and fall of the Hollywood studio system, with major studios controlling a significant portion of film production, distribution, and exhibition. This system began to decline post-war due to various factors, including antitrust legislation that forced studios to divest their theater chains and increased competition.

The late 1930s and early 1940s were a transformative period for Hollywood, marked by technological innovations, shifts in audience preferences, and the broader socio-political impact of World War II on the film content and industry at large

War-Time Cinema

A	R	A	W	K	R	Z	H	P	M	U	I	R	T	P	W
W	W	S	M	S	B	H	I	F	P	O	H	Z	G	L	S
J	R	G	D	V	I	C	T	O	R	Y	I	N	I	X	M
K	E	I	U	P	A	T	R	I	O	T	I	S	M	F	D
B	P	C	E	G	S	H	O	D	P	W	A	L	U	L	U
Y	E	Z	N	F	C	T	H	W	A	B	N	R	W	Z	Y
U	L	Q	N	A	E	X	J	K	G	L	E	P	G	L	N
R	Z	C	U	A	T	N	F	M	A	K	W	L	O	Y	Z
L	S	N	X	H	C	S	S	M	N	Y	S	E	D	C	S
O	F	A	J	O	U	A	I	T	D	W	R	I	J	R	A
X	A	C	N	A	L	B	A	S	A	C	E	O	X	F	Q
F	G	X	Z	C	W	E	D	O	E	H	E	F	C	A	U
S	S	C	F	N	L	N	S	A	G	R	L	B	F	L	U
X	Z	W	I	H	O	I	Z	G	Q	V	S	H	F	D	Z
A	B	D	R	B	F	Q	M	X	F	C	I	Q	Q	K	C
I	T	G	M	F	D	U	U	Y	D	Y	E	N	E	L	P

SOLUTION ON PAGE 140

PROPAGANDA   **RESISTANCE**   **PATRIOTISM**   **RIEFENSTAHL**   **CASABLANCA**
TRIUMPH   **VICTORY**   **NEWSREELS**   **AXIS**   **BONDS**

International Cinema of the Era

J	D	B	R	M	S	I	N	O	I	S	S	E	R	P	X	E	O
H	V	M	B	R	G	E	I	R	V	D	D	N	L	T	N	T	D
U	F	V	X	Y	B	X	E	P	R	H	K	A	A	L	D	U	K
L	G	S	E	M	W	A	T	P	Y	X	C	L	J	C	O	Y	Q
F	U	Q	Y	S	L	G	S	T	H	M	A	L	H	O	B	T	Y
A	J	K	B	I	L	O	N	W	R	Q	M	Y	S	T	F	C	N
O	L	Z	S	L	J	Y	E	Y	M	C	A	C	B	N	S	B	D
O	K	M	L	A	O	E	S	S	E	V	B	I	W	A	M	N	I
G	E	U	Y	E	H	R	I	G	L	E	H	M	I	Q	N	N	E
Z	C	F	R	R	K	L	E	L	C	Y	C	I	B	B	F	M	C
N	B	U	Z	O	A	P	O	N	Y	R	X	C	O	H	W	G	J
H	N	P	G	E	S	L	L	B	O	D	L	O	J	I	Z	M	A
J	C	C	R	N	I	A	Y	B	N	I	C	R	M	N	H	Z	S
P	C	R	R	Q	N	Y	W	H	O	G	R	H	S	N	N	J	O
E	U	P	G	G	Q	K	M	A	V	S	O	B	S	L	M	F	E
S	N	H	P	O	X	H	W	Q	N	V	J	Z	B	Z	F	S	Q
P	B	O	E	A	S	W	B	N	Y	C	H	H	W	X	V	M	N
J	S	O	O	C	J	K	R	N	C	H	Y	B	W	F	Z	J	C

SOLUTION ON PAGE 140

EXPRESSIONISM   NEOREALISM   KUROSAWA   EISENSTEIN   RENOIR
SURREALISM   REALISM   OZU   BICYCLE   LANG

Rudolf Klein-Rogge and Alfred Abel with Maria's Robot in a still from "Metropolis" Dir. Fritz Lang (1927)

METROPOLIS

"Metropolis," directed by Fritz Lang in 1927, stands as one of the most influential masterpieces of the silent film era and a foundational piece in the science fiction genre. Set in a dystopian futuristic city, the film depicts a stratified society where the workers live in miserable conditions in the lower levels, while the elite enjoy opulence at the heights. The plot revolves around Freder, the son of Joh Fredersen, who is the ruling magnate of Metropolis, and his awakening to social injustice after falling in love with Maria, a worker who preaches reconciliation between social strata through the heart.

The production of "Metropolis" was monumental for its time, with an unprecedented budget that funded spectacular sets, thousands of extras, and innovative special effects. The film introduced revolutionary visual techniques, including the use of the Schüfftan technique to create optical illusions, a precursor to modern special effects.

The artistic design of "Metropolis," influenced by movements such as German Expressionism and Art Deco, has left an indelible mark on cinema and popular culture. The image of the robot Maria, for example, became a cinema icon and has inspired numerous works in subsequent decades, from movies to music and art.

The biblical references and reflection on the sentiments following World War I in the film added depth to its narrative, exploring themes of industrialization, class struggle, and the search for humanity within a mechanized society.

Because of this, the initial reception of "Metropolis" was mixed. Its political message was controversial, and reviews varied from awe at its aesthetic vision to confusion about its plot. Over time, however, the film was re-evaluated and is now considered not only a technical achievement but also a profound reflection on industrialization, social class, and humanity, becoming a cult piece of the seventh art.

Over the years, "Metropolis" has undergone cuts and restorations, leading to multiple versions. The search for the original version, which was believed lost, has been a topic of fascination for both film historians and fans. In 2008, an almost complete copy was found in Buenos Aires, Argentina, allowing for the most complete restoration to date, presented in 2010.

"Metropolis" transcends its time not only as a technical milestone but also as a work of art that raises questions about progress, technology, and humanity, themes that remain relevant in the 21st century. The film demonstrates the power of cinema to explore complex ideas and provoke reflection, solidifying Fritz Lang's legacy as one of the medium's most important visionaries.

Key Films of the Golden Age

```
I  M  X  Z  S  M  T  L  Q  G  X  I  F  C  J
K  Z  E  M  W  K  H  E  P  N  D  W  K  O  E
C  W  M  T  M  B  T  T  S  A  M  D  L  A  J
U  U  M  F  R  D  Z  S  F  T  N  M  Y  G  Z
D  U  U  G  G  O  L  L  N  I  C  J  H  W  S
S  Z  Q  T  A  N  P  S  W  M  J  D  N  C  T
X  B  M  K  T  W  S  O  M  E  R  N  H  F  A
E  Y  H  O  F  K  C  P  L  S  G  V  D  R  G
G  A  E  S  A  E  F  H  A  I  G  Q  A  U  E
N  S  T  E  P  S  N  O  W  M  S  K  P  S  C
O  A  J  G  W  U  C  S  F  D  L  X  C  S  O
K  T  J  O  X  O  Q  O  Y  S  V  X  C  L  A
G  Z  C  I  R  W  L  R  N  J  T  M  A  C  C
C  U  L  U  C  G  A  U  O  A  C  X  P  O  H
E  I  S  C  I  T  I  Z  E  N  L  X  W  K  A
```

SOLUTION ON PAGE 140

| METROPOLIS | STEPS | SNOW | STAGECOACH | DUCK |
| CITIZEN | WIND | KONG | TIMES | OZ |

Douglas Fairbanks Hosting the First Oscars Ceremony at the Hollywood Roosevelt Hotel in 1929

The First Oscars Ceremony

The inaugural Oscars ceremony in 1929 at the Hollywood Roosevelt Hotel marked a defining moment not only in recognizing the cinematic achievements of the time but also in establishing a tradition that would endure and evolve over the coming decades. Orchestrated by Douglas Fairbanks, the event brought together Hollywood's elite in a spirit of camaraderie, heralding the dawn of what would become the pinnacle of acknowledgment in the film industry.

Louis B. Mayer's vision in creating the Oscars was to unify the diverse branches of the industry and foster a culture of excellence, a legacy that endures to this day. The meticulous planning of the ceremony, including the trophy's design by Cedric Gibbons, reflected a commitment to prestige and distinction. The trophy's figure, inspired by the stance of Mexican actor and director Emilio 'El Indio' Fernández, would become one of the most iconic and recognizable symbols of cinema.

Over time, the Oscar statuette's design, minimally altered from its inception except for material needs during World War II and minor adjustments to its base in 1945 and 2016, remains an emblem of achievement and recognition. This timeless design and its significance have inspired countless awards worldwide, cementing its place as one of the most coveted and iconic trophies in the art and entertainment world.

The evening was highlighted by a diversity of awards, from performances to technical achievements, showcasing the richness and versatility of cinema during that period. Films like "Wings" and "Sunrise" not only received the highest honors but also foreshadowed the caliber of works to be celebrated in future Oscar editions.

Unique moments from this inaugural ceremony, such as the special acknowledgment given to Charlie Chaplin, underscored the Academy's capacity to appreciate significant contributions beyond established categories. This openness to recognizing art in all its forms has been a pillar of the Oscars over the years.

Looking back, the first Oscars ceremony was not just a retrospective event but a declaration about the future of cinema, setting a standard for celebrating both the art and craft of filmmaking. Over the years, the awards have mirrored changes in the industry, aesthetic trends, and technological innovations, always with a spirit of excellence.

From that initial gathering at the Hollywood Roosevelt Hotel, the Oscars have grown in magnitude and splendor, always retaining the essence of that inaugural ceremony. Each Oscar presentation resonates with the spirit of 1929, reminding us of cinema's power to inspire, unite, and elevate, celebrating not just cinematic achievements but also the continuous evolution and rich diversity of the art of film.

Industry Changes

D	E	S	B	A	R	B	L	E	R	U	T	A	E	F	S
D	S	F	R	A	T	S	V	M	B	K	P	V	Q	D	P
B	P	K	N	Q	V	C	T	O	L	K	C	A	B	F	T
N	F	R	O	N	H	F	H	N	V	A	Z	A	E	P	Y
U	B	V	E	K	U	V	R	E	Y	F	G	V	G	M	U
L	T	G	D	M	E	D	J	P	D	W	H	L	N	Z	C
D	C	O	O	P	I	G	P	K	Y	E	D	U	I	K	V
A	M	I	L	O	S	E	A	I	P	M	K	L	K	Z	O
Q	E	D	E	V	D	P	R	T	H	Y	E	F	O	R	P
X	C	U	K	A	Y	K	A	E	S	B	F	L	O	G	I
T	G	T	C	R	T	H	S	B	Y	D	N	L	B	S	X
J	X	S	I	M	V	D	R	T	A	G	N	W	J	O	O
I	V	R	N	M	J	P	G	B	H	Q	V	U	M	J	F
O	E	D	U	C	T	S	B	T	I	Q	F	I	O	I	C
Z	E	R	J	O	D	D	A	L	A	D	Q	J	U	S	X
X	X	A	A	V	B	H	P	O	A	I	Y	S	N	H	E

SOLUTION ON PAGE 140

NICKELODEON **SOUNDSTAGE** **PREMIERE** **BACKLOT** **FEATURE**
GOLDWYN   **BOOKING**   **STUDIO**   **STAR**   **HAYS**

Walt Disney drawing Mickey Mouse

Early Animation & Cartoons

The history of early animation films begins with iconic figures like Mickey Mouse, created by Walt Disney and Ub Iwerks, who made his first appearance in "Steamboat Willie" in 1928. This short film, notable for being one of the first with synchronized sound, established Mickey Mouse as a beloved character and paved the way for future innovation in animation.

Following Mickey's success, Disney continued to innovate by introducing other animated characters and utilizing Technicolor technology, bringing color to the big screen with "Flowers and Trees" in 1932. This short film not only won an Oscar but also marked the beginning of a new era in color animation.

As Disney led the way, other studios and creators also contributed to the growing field of animation. Characters like Betty Boop, created by Max Fleischer, debuted in 1930 and became symbols of the era, known for their unique style and appeal.

Popeye the Sailor, another iconic character from Fleischer Studios, first appeared in 1929 in the "Thimble Theatre" comic strip and then transitioned to the big screen in 1933. Popeye's popularity quickly soared, thanks to his unique personality and spinach-fueled adventures.

The 1930s also saw the birth of other characters and animated series, such as Warner Bros' Looney Tunes, which debuted in 1930. Characters like Bugs Bunny and Daffy Duck eventually became central figures in the series, beloved for their humor and antics.

This period also witnessed the first feature-length animated film, Disney's "Snow White and the Seven Dwarfs" in 1937, which demonstrated that animation could support complex and emotionally resonant plots, appealing to audiences of all ages.

In summary, the early animated films and characters that emerged during this era were instrumental in the development of animation as an art form and entertainment medium. With characters ranging from Mickey Mouse and Betty Boop to Popeye and the Looney Tunes, this golden age of animation laid the groundwork for decades of innovation and creativity to follow.

Early Animation & Cartoons

M	R	W	P	Q	X	N	L	B	D	L	G	W	A
J	K	E	O	U	S	N	O	K	Q	H	B	D	P
L	Y	M	H	B	X	P	M	Z	A	E	K	R	Z
T	B	H	K	C	G	G	E	R	T	I	E	G	M
S	Z	K	A	S	S	Y	T	T	S	H	F	I	V
L	Y	Z	I	I	E	I	Y	T	C	I	S	D	S
Y	X	U	T	P	S	D	E	M	E	J	L	G	L
V	K	H	O	E	E	A	G	L	T	O	N	L	D
X	N	P	Z	X	M	K	T	W	F	X	B	T	Y
U	S	R	I	B	I	Y	E	N	S	I	D	I	W
E	W	H	O	N	C	L	L	O	A	L	D	W	M
J	K	A	P	I	K	A	E	W	K	F	H	Y	U
P	T	O	T	S	E	F	D	F	C	Y	L	J	J
R	J	T	L	M	Y	T	A	Z	U	S	E	M	C

SOLUTION ON PAGE 141

FANTASIA **POPEYE** **STEAMBOAT** **FLEISCHER** **FELIX**
DISNEY **BETTY** **MICKEY** **GERTIE** **SILLY**

John Ford. The Portraitist of the Human Condition

John Ford, whose real name was John Martin Feeney, is an iconic and influential figure in the history of both American and global cinema. Born on February 1, 1894, in Cape Elizabeth, Maine, Ford began his career in silent films. He preferred to be called Jack, and under this name, he started in 1914 as a jack-of-all-trades at the Universal studios, under the protectively aggressive shadow of his brother Francis, from whom he learned the ABCs of the trade. No one could have predicted that he would become one of the most recognized and respected directors of Hollywood's classic era. Throughout his career, Ford directed over 140 films, spanning a wide range of genres, though he is best known for his Westerns and his profound collaborations with actors such as John Wayne and Henry Fonda.

Ford moved to California in 1914, where he initially worked for his brother, Francis Ford, also a director and actor. He soon began to establish himself as a director, and his early films, such as "The Iron Horse" (1924) and "3 Bad Men" (1926), showcased his ability to tell complex stories and his affinity for the vast American landscapes, which would become a stylistic signature in his work.

As cinema transitioned from silent to sound, Ford adapted seamlessly, demonstrating a narrative prowess that transcended dialogue. His film "The Informer" (1935), based on the novel by Liam O'Flaherty about the Irish Civil War, earned him his first Academy Award for Best Director. However, it was with "Stagecoach" (1939), starring John Wayne, that Ford revitalized the Western genre and set a new standard for these films, both in terms of narrative and cinematographic technique.

Ford was known for his ability to portray the human condition within the context of American history, often focusing on themes such as community, justice, and morality. This tendency is evident in masterpieces like "The Grapes of Wrath" (1940), an adaptation of John Steinbeck's book exploring the hardships of a family during the Great Depression, and "How Green Was My Valley" (1941), which narrates the life of a mining community in Wales, for which he won his third Oscar for Best Director.

During World War II, Ford served in the U.S. Navy and directed several documentaries for the government, including "The Battle of Midway" (1942), which captured real footage of the battle and earned him an Academy Award in the Best Documentary category.

After the war, Ford continued to explore the American West with iconic titles like "My Darling Clementine" (1946), "Fort Apache" (1948), "She Wore a Yellow Ribbon" (1949), and "The Searchers" (1956), cementing his place as a master of the genre. His ability to blend action, drama, and moments of lightness, along with his iconic use of locations in Monument Valley, contributed to his enduring legacy.

Ford also explored other genres, such as comedy in "The Quiet Man" (1952), set in Ireland and starring John Wayne and Maureen O'Hara, for which he won his fourth Oscar for Best Director. His last significant film, "The Man Who Shot Liberty Valance" (1962), is often seen as a reflection on the end of the traditional Western era and the nature of legend and myth in American history.

Although he was not actually one-eyed, he always wore a patch over one of his eyes. He occasionally wore it in 1934 to recover from cataract surgery. Thereafter, he accustomed to wearing it in public as an eccentricity, though he often switched it from one eye to the other.

John Ford passed away on August 31, 1973, in Palm Desert, California. His influence on cinema is immeasurable, not only for his visual and technical style but also for his deep understanding of narrative and his ability to capture the essence of the American experience. Ford left a legacy that has inspired generations of filmmakers, and his work continues to be a reference point in the study of cinematic art.

Great Film Directors of the 1930s

Q	P	O	Z	P	E	K	Q	L	I	V	F	H	Q
L	U	G	Y	H	O	K	B	M	Q	T	N	E	N
B	U	I	D	R	I	N	C	H	A	P	L	I	N
M	X	C	L	I	K	T	F	O	R	D	U	H	R
H	L	S	Q	P	H	V	C	Y	P	Q	B	O	V
P	T	O	E	R	S	Y	W	H	A	P	I	K	L
O	R	A	I	L	O	Y	S	A	C	G	T	P	P
D	C	S	M	O	L	L	A	N	G	O	S	H	F
A	I	E	Y	E	H	E	U	C	N	Q	C	C	F
M	I	C	R	K	S	K	W	A	H	V	H	K	I
P	W	S	L	O	A	B	E	Z	B	D	D	F	Z
O	T	X	N	P	Z	L	K	G	S	B	Z	G	V
Q	Q	L	L	C	F	V	X	F	H	G	S	R	J
G	M	M	C	M	O	H	P	F	E	V	I	A	N

SOLUTION ON PAGE 141

| HITCHCOCK | LUBITSCH | CHAPLIN | HAWKS | FORD |
| WELLES | WYLER | CAPRA | LANG | LEAN |

Iconic 1930s Film Characters

```
W H F T J E C G S E M L O H F C V
Q T T O D E Z J A D S N L J M W F
H V H Y N G T R E S G V A X S R S
K G S A Y B S T A G U O Q Z L F F
Y O A K Q H V D E J Y K O F R C I
X I D D L G L G S L B F W Y L A G
O M X W O A X S H O R R O Z L E T
I Y G G V B O Y D A E A W U C Y K
L R N S O N B H N Q M D C A N G Z
X O T I V Q H K G U O A Q S M H D
K R L M R B E O Q W R C B D B S F
M C W D N N K N L D X J E R W T A
F E R Q S I O S T V J B A J K B V
O Y H T O R O D L O G K S E S E V
C W E R O O P R Q J H H J F B C W
B I T H K W F C D B M J E A O N E
N G T R T S L X Z H B O I J V P U
```

SOLUTION ON PAGE 141

FRANKENSTEIN **DOROTHY** **SCARLETT** **HOLMES** **GATSBY**
DRACULA **TARZAN** **ZORRO** **RHETT** **KONG**

Scene from "The Wizard of Oz" Dir. Victor Fleming (1939)

Did You Know This About "The Wizard of Oz"?

Innovative Special Effects: Beyond the horses colored with flavored gelatin, the movie used cutting-edge techniques for its time, including the tornado, created with a 35-foot-long muslin stocking that was spun around while dirt, dust, and wind were blown against it, creating a convincing effect for audiences.

Last-Minute Casting Changes: Buddy Ebsen, initially cast as the Tin Man, had to be replaced by Jack Haley due to a severe allergic reaction to the aluminum powder in his makeup. This near-fatal experience led to a switch to an aluminum paste for Haley, though it still resulted in an eye infection for the actor.

Actors' Ages: Margaret Hamilton, the Wicked Witch of the West, was only 36 years old, contrary to her character's old hag depiction. Interestingly, Billie Burke, who played Glinda and appeared younger, was 54 years old.

Toto, the Canine Star: Toto, played by a female Cairn Terrier named Terry, earned $125 a week, more than many of the Munchkin actors. Terry had a successful career in movies until her death in 1945.

Rumors and Myths: There's a rumor that a Munchkin committed suicide during filming and that his body can be seen in one of the scenes, but this has been debunked and attributed to the shadows of birds brought in to create a more realistic woodland setting.

Costume and Makeup Changes: Judy Garland started filming with a blonde wig and heavy baby-doll makeup, but interim director George Cukor opted for a more natural appearance. Also, the worn coat used by Professor Marvel/The Wizard turned out to be a thrift store find that once belonged to "Oz" author L. Frank Baum, with his name sewn into the garment.

On-Set Challenges: The Wicked Witch actress, Margaret Hamilton, suffered severe burns in the scene where she disappears into a cloud of smoke, and her stunt double was also injured during the skywriting sequence.

The Creative Process: Bringing "The Wizard of Oz" to the big screen required five directors and 14 writers, underscoring the complexity and challenges of bringing this ambitious production to life.

Breakthroughs in Film Sound & Music

```
C D C Y T H E K Z M O Z M H T
S F V C S O U N D T R A C K C
B V I N A N G A M J C P W H Z
K V L Y E L O F O X H V R I G
S K G S B P L Y W L E N K N T
B Y Y O P L A L N J S R I B C
A N H C I A I Z O S T D S D L
N F K R A Y D T L C R B I J S
U R B K E B S C F O A G T Y V
M U S I C A L U C R J H A H D
L I A V Y C B E D E E X K Z K
J M F T W K R R B M H O Q C L
K Q G E N O X P E A I F O W Q
U D R G Z P N N T G L J K S S
K Z R U G N Y G V Q G D T B W
```

SOLUTION ON PAGE 141

ORCHESTRA   RECORDING   SOUNDTRACK   THEME   SCORE
PLAYBACK   MUSICAL   DIALOGUE   FOLEY   SYNC

The Great Depression

The Great Depression, sparked by the 1929 stock market crash, plunged the film industry, like many others, into a challenging economic situation. During this period, people's ability to spend on entertainment drastically decreased, leading to a significant drop in cinema attendance. However, despite these challenges, the 1930s are also known as the "Golden Age of Hollywood," characterized by the production of some of the most iconic films in history.

To combat the decline in audiences, film studios implemented several innovative strategies. One such tactic was the double-feature system, which offered two films for the price of one, enhancing the perceived value for viewers. Additionally, newsreels before the films and low-budget "B movies" were introduced, often screened as the second film in a double feature.

The industry also saw the birth and consolidation of genres that offered escapism or a reflection of the era's struggles. Musicals and comedies became popular for their ability to provide relief and joy, while gangster films reflected the darker reality of life during the Depression.

The introduction of sound cinema in the late 1920s also played a crucial role during this time, providing a new cinematic experience that attracted audiences. Technological innovation continued with the development of better filming techniques, special effects, and the use of Technicolor, which added visual appeal to the films.

Despite economic hardships, the 1930s witnessed the creation of many masterpieces and the rise of iconic stars. Films like "Gone with the Wind" (1939), "The Wizard of Oz" (1939), and "King Kong" (1933) not only survived the Depression but became timeless classics. Stars such as Clark Gable, Bette Davis, and Greta Garbo became symbols of an era that, despite adversity, flourished artistically.

The resilience of the film industry during the Great Depression demonstrates the importance of cinema as a form of escape and its ability to adapt and thrive even in the most challenging times. This era left a lasting legacy in terms of innovation, creativity, and the consolidation of cinema as an essential part of global culture and entertainment.

The Impact of the Great Depression on Cinema

```
Z Q V R X E K T R A F C K L B
R J R O O P Y S E C B L O N I
U E D G A F Y F Y K Y H W X P
U D Q E I E G Q G B C H M V Q
M U H M Y H Y H P E T I A B X
S C A H B O Y T H R I F T Y R
X C G F C Z L T R K H Y I D Y
A I N V C X V P R E R Z N J U
R U S V R S G U M L V B E W Z
F G Q M S W V N T E U O E W D
V T C V L Y U N S Y N P P N J
Y N B D M A X C Y B S U B J A
R X D L G L A I R E S T R M U
T S H A Q P C Q O J A R T E U
Y B P X E E E W A B G H J S F
```

SOLUTION ON PAGE 142

UNEMPLOYED   BERKELEY   POVERTY   THRIFTY   SERIAL
MATINEE   ESCAPE   TICKET   CHEAP   BUSBY

Major Film Studios of the Golden Age

S	U	H	U	N	I	V	E	R	S	A	L	J	Z	L	D	H	O
C	A	W	V	R	U	Q	Y	D	T	W	R	T	C	E	V	A	I
H	W	N	Z	O	R	Q	O	R	G	P	J	I	F	G	A	T	B
X	W	A	L	A	O	D	U	K	A	G	L	Q	A	L	I	S	I
Z	T	M	F	Y	N	J	D	N	E	B	V	K	I	F	H	M	C
I	B	S	O	T	I	Z	S	E	U	L	W	E	P	N	D	N	D
J	L	C	K	L	Z	W	H	P	S	Y	S	E	L	R	G	P	M
S	R	D	P	Q	X	C	E	N	P	I	X	F	X	T	M	A	D
K	D	W	W	S	E	R	U	T	C	I	P	O	I	D	A	R	T
L	I	I	P	E	A	V	F	N	M	K	Y	X	O	H	A	Q	H
O	K	L	S	W	W	W	M	N	U	Z	E	D	O	S	T	I	E	K
H	V	B	J	N	F	Y	G	O	Y	F	G	D	W	Z	B	V	M
L	V	G	E	S	E	M	F	M	A	R	G	O	N	O	M	Z	O
N	A	L	J	E	U	Y	C	A	N	C	W	H	R	K	U	E	Y
X	K	V	W	A	R	N	E	R	M	L	F	S	K	J	L	M	F
M	C	F	H	W	L	B	P	A	R	S	Y	D	J	V	O	B	U
P	R	Z	B	P	O	C	S	P	J	T	Y	T	Q	V	C	C	Y
W	R	M	T	T	R	P	L	E	I	F	V	I	Q	T	B	Y	T

SOLUTION ON PAGE 142

PARAMOUNT COLUMBIA UNIVERSAL RADIOPICTURES MONOGRAM
DISNEY WARNER REPUBLIC FOX MGM

Image of Alfred Hitchcock and François Truffaut at Universal Pictures studios in 1962

Did you know that Truffaut was a Critic?

François Truffaut, an iconic figure in the world of cinema, transcended from his role as a passionate critic to become a pioneering director, leaving an indelible mark on the cinematic landscape. He began his career at "Cahiers du Cinéma," where he defended auteur theory and criticized conventional French cinema of his time, laying the groundwork for the French New Wave. Alongside contemporaries like Jean-Luc Godard and Eric Rohmer, Truffaut revolutionized filmmaking with a playful approach to narrative and a preference for shooting on real locations, influencing later filmmakers such as Steven Spielberg, Bong Joon-ho, Greta Gerwig, and Wes Anderson.

Truffaut's dialogue with cinema extended beyond his own directing. His engagement with Alfred Hitchcock's work, especially through the extensive interviews compiled in "Hitchcock/Truffaut" (1966), demonstrated his deep respect for the craft and his desire to delve into the complexities of filmmaking. "The 400 Blows," his directorial debut, exemplifies his unique approach, blending personal storytelling and technical innovation, earning him international recognition.

The interaction between Truffaut and Hitchcock at Universal Pictures in 1962, where they held a profound conversation about cinema for a week, is a notable episode in film history. Although these talks were initially expected to be published quickly, they did not become a book until four years later. Helen Scott's presence as a translator facilitated this cultural exchange, and the editing process underscored Truffaut's intention to present Hitchcock not just as a filmmaker but as an artistically oriented auteur.

This encounter not only highlights the importance of editing and presentation in creating a legacy but also illustrates how the visions of two influential cinema figures can merge to offer new perspectives on the art of filmmaking. "Hitchcock/Truffaut" remains an invaluable resource for filmmakers and enthusiasts, providing deep insight into the techniques and thoughts behind some of Hitchcock's most iconic films.

Truffaut's trajectory from critic to director exemplifies a unique transition from critique to creation, displaying a deep cinematic knowledge that enriched his work behind the camera. His passion for film and innovative approach made him one of the most significant directors of his generation, with a legacy that continues to be highly esteemed in the global film industry.

Notable Film Critics & Theorists

```
J K R V J K N A T C F W H L H
N F N K D R A D O G L H K I Y
M M B M P E P H C X S O G M G
G D U L U K A X Z X I T U G D
P C X Z N E I B A B R P X Q R
S K K K Q I C A A M Y A L G A
C A N K M X E B L A E D M A
R I R X S E O T J A A N I F E
I L N E X R Z R S K Z Z P P X
Y T R N U S N U L N E I S R G
D I X Z C A T F M I E H N R A
Q W K I T R C F U I G S Y V W
L A O P J R O A N S A G I G T
P G I X X I V U R M S T K E H
N O R L K S R T O K Z B T Q B
```

SOLUTION ON PAGE 142

TRUFFAUT	**EISENSTEIN**	**ARNHEIM**	**KRACAUER**	**AGEE**
GODARD	**BALAZS**	**SARRIS**	**BAZIN**	**KAEL**

Advances in Film Technology

S	W	Y	T	M	O	G	H	L	Z	E	A	V	B	P
F	O	G	Z	A	D	J	G	Q	S	X	Q	P	H	A
V	L	D	N	D	U	Y	K	L	D	F	X	B	E	T
M	Z	R	W	I	J	P	M	L	O	B	R	E	R	N
D	I	W	B	X	T	R	W	A	L	Q	A	S	L	Z
E	N	C	M	O	Q	H	Y	W	L	U	C	F	N	K
R	D	U	R	T	Z	X	G	F	Y	T	P	S	Z	Z
E	S	I	O	O	L	E	J	I	R	A	U	A	S	O
W	D	O	T	S	P	D	R	O	L	O	C	N	V	E
Y	F	H	C	I	I	H	C	U	E	M	C	A	V	X
P	O	W	E	Z	N	A	O	A	T	Z	R	E	J	L
D	T	C	J	J	M	G	E	N	A	R	C	Z	D	Y
Z	G	W	O	E	W	C	R	J	E	T	D	I	H	P
K	O	G	R	U	B	R	Q	N	I	Y	V	O	Y	X
L	B	A	P	Q	Q	B	M	O	V	I	O	L	A	P

SOLUTION ON PAGE 142

MOVIOLA	PROJECTOR	CAMERA	MICROPHONE	LIGHTING
COLOR	CRANE	DOLLY	SOUND	EDITING

Landmark Films of the Era

L	B	F	M	V	H	Y	Y	R	M	E	I	Q	D	N
S	U	A	B	S	C	F	C	C	N	D	E	P	T	A
O	L	Y	M	P	I	A	V	V	O	B	M	E	K	L
J	H	E	A	R	M	L	H	F	F	Q	S	H	A	U
T	M	F	G	I	G	C	O	X	Y	G	C	S	H	U
H	K	E	L	N	X	J	F	P	M	T	K	U	T	N
O	N	L	Y	H	A	H	L	O	O	U	R	A	S	L
N	E	Q	K	W	M	O	C	N	D	R	W	S	I	U
R	E	K	U	I	O	U	I	U	E	A	T	Z	J	W
S	X	N	V	Y	T	N	X	M	R	X	Z	E	I	J
S	M	G	N	M	L	E	P	A	N	Y	I	R	M	E
B	S	T	Q	E	V	P	K	Y	L	F	N	W	R	S
U	S	C	S	H	C	A	O	C	E	G	A	T	S	J
S	F	Y	C	G	U	H	L	I	K	Q	Y	H	A	E
D	U	C	K	U	G	U	B	D	N	X	S	T	A	A

SOLUTION ON PAGE 143

METROPOLIS   **NINOTCHKA**   **ANGELS**   **STAGECOACH**   **AWARA**
OLYMPIA   **MODERN**   **DUCK**   **CAMILLE**   **ONLY**

CHAPTER TWO
1940-1990

Still frame from the movie "Mrs. Miniver", Dir. William Wyler (1942)

Hollywood during World War II

During World War II, Hollywood played a pivotal role, not just as a means of entertainment but also as a significant contributor to the war effort. The early 1940s saw Hollywood in a state of transition, adapting to the realities of a world at war while still providing the escapism and morale boost that audiences craved.

During this time, Hollywood produced a range of films that reflected the themes of the war, from propaganda films designed to boost morale and patriotic spirit to documentaries and feature films that depicted the heroism and sacrifices of the war. Directors like Frank Capra, known for his "Why We Fight" series, and John Ford, with works such as "They Were Expendable," played key roles in shaping the narrative of the war through cinema.

The impact of these films on American society was profound. They served not only as entertainment but also as a means of educating the public about the stakes of the war and the importance of national unity and support for the troops. Movies like "Casablanca" and "Mrs. Miniver" offered stories of resilience and resistance that resonated with the audiences of the time, encapsulating the ethos of an era defined by global conflict.

Moreover, Hollywood's involvement extended beyond the screen. Many actors and filmmakers joined the military or contributed to the war effort in various capacities, further blurring the lines between the film industry and the war effort. The war also led to technological and narrative innovations in filmmaking, influenced by the need to convey the reality of the conflict and the desire to tell more complex stories.

Overall, the World War II years were a time of significant change and growth for Hollywood, as it navigated the challenges of wartime production and censorship, the shift in audience demands, and the evolving landscape of global politics. The era left an indelible mark on the industry, shaping the future of filmmaking and solidifying cinema's role as a crucial part of American cultural identity.

Hollywood During World War II

```
U I Q S U C V C A Z P K L N Z K
S U C A N T E E N G A X A Y Q L
O L F D O C U M E N T A R Y J X
H B E P G Y O S B A R D L E V E
V Z H E S S N R N O I N F Q N Z
Q X Z S R Y M A M Y O A C A V W
N M I C Q S H W K U T G C Y I F
L H A J R N W I G E I A M O C W
X D H U I C M E N X S P N J T I
X C A D S R I O N A M O H U O N
X R E B L C Q Z B S V R T A R Q
X O L G W E F L L J J P Q B Y O
K K D G D Y A T T S B Q W G O P
J V C U T N W N R S T K R U W G
X D C G C W O S O N M U T Y W P
H I Q A H P Z B S X O Z C E N N
```

SOLUTION ON PAGE 143

| PROPAGANDA | DOCUMENTARY | CANTEEN | CASABLANCA | NOIR |
| VICTORY | PATRIOTISM | BOND | NEWSREELS | USO |

Post-War Cinema

```
N G D M B A M A R D O L E M Z
D E Q G U K F Y I A N S B M A
Q B R N U E V H G D N P D W W
F I I P F I O N R K T J D H
Z G L H T I E F E C X Z L H Y
R C F J R A J T O G R G Y H O
P W L S P H S C R C A Y P G U
X X J L R E H X E I K W R Q L
B D M A W C K M A Z O E E V B
W Z E C T H Y B L C I N W N A
A W T I E M P L I R K J O O Y
Y K H S O A W A S O R U K X M
J R O U E W N T M S Y O T L P
A Y D M L C A D T V N N F O W
L F A G C I C I P E E S D B T
```

SOLUTION ON PAGE 143

NEOREALISM   MELODRAMA   HITCHCOCK   MUSICALS   KUROSAWA
SATIRE   WESTERNS   METHOD   NOIR   EPIC

James Dean

James Dean. An Eternal Icon

James Dean, with his brief yet intense career and tragic end, transcends the category of mere actor to become an eternal icon of popular culture and cinema. His image, marked by a combination of vulnerability, rebellion, and innate charisma, elevates him to a lasting symbol of youth and social discontent.

Born in Indiana, Dean's early life was marked by the loss of his mother, an event that deeply influenced his character and his quest for meaning in acting. This quest led him to New York and, eventually, to Hollywood, where his unique talent quickly set him apart from his contemporaries. Despite his rising fame, Dean remained enigmatic and complex, known for his intensity both on and off the screen.

Onscreen, Dean became the archetype of the youthful anti-hero, particularly with his role in "Rebel Without a Cause." The authenticity of his performance in this and other films, such as "East of Eden" and "Giant," resonated with a generation of youths seeking a voice that reflected their own concerns and disillusionments. Dean embodied a sensibility that went beyond his roles, one that spoke of defiance and an unending search for identity.

Dean's premature death at 24 in a car accident cemented his legendary status. His life and career, though brief, left an indelible impression not only on the film industry but on popular culture as a whole. Dean became a symbol of eternal youth and the struggle against convention, an emblem of rebellion and artistic sensitivity.

Today, Dean is remembered not only for his performances but for what he represents: perpetual youth, unfulfilled promise, and the complexity of the human experience. His image, often replicated but never equaled, continues to inspire actors, filmmakers, and cinephiles around the world. James Dean, in essence, personifies a moment in time where vulnerability and rebellion intertwined, capturing the spirit of an era and resonating across generations.

Golden Age Film Stars

V	M	N	H	G	K	B	E	E	H	Y	Y
R	B	R	A	N	D	O	V	Z	M	Y	D
A	G	U	D	M	U	K	D	O	L	N	X
L	R	B	A	W	G	E	N	Y	A	W	S
S	R	P	N	P	A	R	O	I	T	H	V
S	E	E	K	N	O	L	E	Z	K	N	Y
Q	Q	H	D	E	I	F	O	B	E	U	U
I	X	G	Z	V	R	T	D	O	L	N	Y
P	S	F	I	B	V	F	N	G	L	Z	W
V	F	E	L	C	V	F	S	A	Y	P	V
Z	R	W	T	D	Z	Q	P	R	R	Z	P
F	I	L	X	Q	Y	Q	X	T	H	G	H

SOLUTION ON PAGE 143

| BERGMAN | HEPBURN | MONROE | BRANDO | BOGART |
| GRANT | KELLY | DEAN | WAYNE | OLIVIER |

Orson Welles

Orson "Citizen" Welles

Orson Welles was a monumental figure in film history, known for both his creative genius and his complex, charismatic personality. Born George Orson Welles on May 6, 1915, in Kenosha, Wisconsin, and passing away on October 10, 1985, Welles left an indelible mark on the entertainment world through his contributions to radio, theater, and most significantly, cinema.

Welles began his career in theater before making a name for himself in radio, where his 1938 broadcast of H.G. Wells' "The War of the Worlds," presented as a real news bulletin, caused panic among listeners who believed an actual alien invasion was occurring. This broadcast not only demonstrated his ability to captivate audiences but also his inclination to challenge conventions and explore new forms of storytelling.

However, it is for "Citizen Kane" (1941) that Welles is most remembered and revered. At the age of 25, he wrote, directed, and starred in this film, often cited as one of the greatest of all time. "Citizen Kane" broke new ground in terms of cinematic narrative, cinematography, music, and production design, establishing Welles as a cinematic visionary.

Despite critical success, Welles faced difficulties with Hollywood studios, limiting his ability to carry out projects according to his vision. Nevertheless, he continued to create significant works such as "The Magnificent Ambersons" (1942), "The Lady from Shanghai" (1947), and "Macbeth" (1948). His innovative style and willingness to experiment kept him as an influential figure in auteur cinema.

Welles' influence extends beyond his films; his pioneering approach to storytelling and filmmaking continues to inspire filmmakers worldwide. Despite controversies and challenges in his career, Orson Welles remains a legend whose work challenges, intrigues, and delights audiences generations after his death. His legacy is a testament to his brilliance, indomitable spirit, and unwavering dedication to the art of cinema.

1950s & 1960s Directors

D	R	C	A	S	K	S	N	M	B	S	V	J	G
V	U	M	I	G	F	X	F	V	N	E	W	H	A
U	L	H	Z	G	O	P	Q	U	U	L	W	P	Z
O	T	D	Y	X	X	I	N	X	E	L	F	C	X
A	O	Y	D	J	N	A	M	G	R	E	B	Z	M
P	N	K	Y	M	E	L	H	D	L	W	H	G	S
B	G	T	B	L	K	G	M	L	C	A	O	S	X
A	N	U	O	W	V	C	I	Y	B	D	K	A	U
D	R	A	G	N	I	N	I	A	A	H	P	I	L
X	R	F	P	Y	I	L	I	R	H	K	X	H	C
Z	L	F	Z	V	V	O	D	Y	B	Y	L	H	L
G	I	U	G	F	V	D	N	E	C	U	E	D	O
W	G	R	N	P	N	S	M	I	R	K	K	H	J
L	T	T	L	L	H	P	X	J	H	M	A	K	G

SOLUTION ON PAGE 144

TRUFFAUT   **ANTONIONI**   **BERGMAN**   **FELLINI**   **GODARD**
KUBRICK   **WELLES**   **WILDER**   **RAY**   **LEAN**

Still frame from the film "Seven Samurai" Dir. Akira Kurosawa (1954)

Seven Samurai

"Seven Samurai" ("七人の侍", "Shichinin no Samurai") is a masterpiece of Japanese cinema directed by Akira Kurosawa in 1954. Set in 16th-century Japan, this epic film tells the story of a small village of farmers who hire seven rōnin (masterless samurai) to protect their village from bandits threatening to plunder their crops each year.

The plot revolves around the relationship between the samurai and the villagers, exploring themes of honor, duty, sacrifice, and the social gap between warriors and peasants. Kurosawa uses a three-part narrative structure: the assembly of the samurai team, the interaction between the samurai and the villagers, and the epic final battle against the bandits.

"Seven Samurai" is notable for its innovative cinematographic techniques, such as the use of slow motion in combat scenes, and for its profound narrative and well-developed characters. Kurosawa employs weather, especially rain, as a narrative element that adds emotional and dramatic intensity to the battle scenes.

The film is not only one of the most influential in Kurosawa's filmography but also in world cinema. Its "assemble the team" narrative structure has been adopted and adapted by countless movies and genres, from westerns to science fiction. "Seven Samurai" directly inspired the 1960 classic western "The Magnificent Seven," and its influence extends to works like "Star Wars" and other hero group narratives.

"Seven Samurai" was both a critical and commercial success and continues to be revered as one of the greatest films of all time. Kurosawa's ability to tell complex stories with emotional depth, combined with masterful direction and compelling performances, makes "Seven Samurai" a timeless and universal cinematic experience.

In summary, "Seven Samurai" stands as not just a cornerstone of Japanese cinema but a significant contribution to global cinema, celebrated for its epic storytelling, memorable characters, and pioneering cinematographic techniques that continue to influence filmmakers around the world.

Iconic Films of the 1950s

J	T	J	T	B	C	V	J	M	A	G	O	J	N
A	B	B	J	O	P	A	C	H	K	D	J	R	P
C	L	Y	K	G	G	P	Y	O	K	X	F	K	G
V	K	L	P	S	Q	O	C	Z	Q	J	M	Y	K
F	E	K	I	Y	U	N	N	S	I	P	G	A	R
B	E	R	O	Z	O	N	M	T	V	G	L	M	Y
T	Y	O	T	C	D	N	S	R	R	E	W	H	P
E	H	J	X	I	Z	O	Z	E	B	E	O	F	B
U	H	N	Y	A	G	M	G	E	T	E	D	E	H
Z	F	G	T	O	E	O	R	T	C	J	N	V	S
I	E	B	R	B	X	H	D	C	H	H	I	F	C
A	H	F	B	L	D	S	Y	A	U	P	W	W	B
Q	B	E	T	K	B	A	B	R	E	V	I	R	I
A	Q	S	A	M	U	R	A	I	A	P	Z	T	B

SOLUTION ON PAGE 144

GODZILLA **VERTIGO** **SAMURAI** **STREETCAR** **RASHOMON**
SUNSET   **RIVER**   **REBEL**   **WINDOW**   **BENHUR**

Rise of Television

A	C	I	B	L	L	I	T	L	J	U	J	R	P
G	M	Y	Y	U	K	R	N	C	A	B	L	E	P
H	K	H	S	N	T	M	E	H	Q	H	T	P	P
R	Q	E	X	N	Q	E	W	O	F	B	X	M	A
K	B	T	A	J	J	V	S	I	P	P	Q	L	K
R	R	D	C	Y	V	U	W	E	D	C	G	P	J
C	O	O	I	W	A	A	O	O	X	I	G	O	R
W	A	F	W	O	R	N	S	M	Y	H	Y	T	W
T	D	V	I	T	I	C	O	L	O	R	E	P	H
O	C	Z	G	V	E	C	A	G	K	T	W	Q	R
E	A	J	I	L	T	N	P	X	O	G	W	I	D
X	S	F	P	I	Y	D	G	M	J	L	J	C	Y
F	T	C	S	E	I	R	E	S	K	E	X	S	P
D	J	L	L	J	B	R	B	E	H	F	U	Z	Q

SOLUTION ON PAGE 144

BROADCAST   NETWORK   CABLE   VARIETY   REMOTE
SITCOM   SERIES   SOAP   NEWS   COLOR

New Wave Movements

```
D F V L C E I K U R K C H B U
D U B Z P L D C G F X D H A P
E R C H B X C R L A L T S U H
T B X T E F O U D G W V I S J
F K W U T D D A B R Y C L T K
H I F Q R T X U I A O R O R N
U G D J Z V W E S E N A P A J
S L L E W F G E B A Q K I L C
Z X U S F E G S S R T L F I R
V M S D R F L V M X I T C A G
F Q C M E Q J E V Z C T C N U
Z N A R N A I L A T I N I D O
P N L P C V J R P Z C L J S M
T V F S H Y B D D C C Z E C H
W J V A R W O X D O Y N R W B
```

SOLUTION ON PAGE 144

AUSTRALIAN   JAPANESE   ITALIAN   BRITISH   BRAZILIAN
GERMAN   POLISH   CUBAN   CZECH   FRENCH

Sci-Fi & Fantasy of the 1960s

V	J	H	L	Q	R	W	B	M	I	I	J	I	D	S
E	T	T	X	J	L	A	G	J	W	M	T	G	U	E
P	N	Q	O	N	A	L	I	E	N	M	E	O	D	A
R	L	G	J	B	Y	L	L	R	C	F	O	S	I	B
R	W	A	A	P	O	E	T	W	B	H	O	Q	I	L
T	M	L	N	A	G	R	S	Y	M	G	Z	A	K	H
O	H	J	V	E	C	A	P	S	K	O	Z	T	S	D
O	U	X	U	R	T	B	P	J	Y	J	R	R	M	Z
U	U	I	G	U	I	R	J	E	X	D	O	E	V	G
O	Y	S	A	T	N	A	F	E	S	I	O	K	Q	V
V	Q	J	H	U	I	B	F	H	K	W	E	K	W	E
L	Z	E	F	F	L	E	C	E	Q	D	T	Y	O	F
H	E	A	Y	G	X	I	H	U	M	W	T	F	L	Q
L	Z	R	T	G	X	T	Y	C	I	W	V	H	D	H
V	K	W	Q	W	J	B	L	M	B	V	P	Y	K	W

SOLUTION ON PAGE 145

BARBARELLA   TREK   FANTASY   ROBOT   FUTURE
ODYSSEY   APES   PLANET   ALIEN   SPACE

Natalie Wood and Richard Beymer are Maria and Tony in "West Side Story" Dir. by Jerome Robbins and Robert Wise (1961)

Music & Cinema

The musical cinema, which shone with particular intensity from the 1950s to the 1970s, marked an unforgettable chapter in the history of film. This era, characterized by its visual opulence and elaborate choreographies, became the backdrop for some of Hollywood's most iconic productions.

In the 1950s, musical cinema found new life with films that stood out not only for their musical numbers but also for the depth of their stories and the quality of their performances. This decade saw the birth of classics like "Singin' in the Rain" (1952), where Gene Kelly, Debbie Reynolds, and Donald O'Connor displayed a feast of talent, combining comedy, drama, and impressive choreography, especially in Kelly's iconic scene dancing under torrential rain.

Fred Astaire, another titan of the genre, continued his legacy in this era, bringing elegance and effortless grace to the big screen. Films like "Funny Face" (1957), in which Astaire co-starred with Audrey Hepburn, showcased the musical cinema's ability to blend fashion, romance, and spectacular numbers, creating a timeless cinematic experience.

As we moved into the 1960s, musical cinema adopted more varied and daring themes. "West Side Story" (1961), an adaptation of Shakespeare's classic "Romeo and Juliet" set in New York, broke molds with its treatment of issues such as racism and urban violence, all framed within an unforgettable score and choreographies that have become genre benchmarks.

The 1970s brought with them a revolution in musical cinema, with titles that explored new aesthetic and narrative directions. "Cabaret" (1972), starring Liza Minnelli, is a perfect example of how the genre adapted to the times, offering a raw yet stylized look at pre-Nazi Germany, combining historical drama with musical performances that stood out for both their content and form.

"Grease" (1978), on the other hand, revived the nostalgia for the 1950s with a modern twist, capturing the spirit of youth and sexual awakening through catchy songs and energetic performances by John Travolta and Olivia Newton-John. This film not only became a milestone for future generations but also demonstrated the versatility and enduring appeal of musical cinema.

This golden era of musical cinema left us a legacy of innovation, spectacle, and emotion, reminding us of the unique power of film to combine visual narrative with music and dance, creating worlds that transcend the screen and stay with us long after the lights come on.

Music & Concert Films

T	K	T	M	A	L	F	F	B	W	S	L	R	S	S	E
M	A	K	M	J	L	A	T	O	W	T	C	B	X	V	A
P	F	T	Z	K	D	B	P	M	H	N	Q	I	A	I	O
I	K	A	L	O	E	J	U	C	P	D	B	V	B	Q	P
A	Y	X	N	P	V	C	X	M	O	U	Z	O	Z	D	R
J	E	D	Q	A	E	Q	A	C	Q	N	P	S	X	L	C
X	E	V	L	V	N	R	U	G	T	K	C	O	R	K	E
W	M	L	A	E	G	M	F	M	Y	S	Z	E	P	H	D
O	P	D	V	U	E	R	S	O	P	B	H	E	R	C	U
O	D	I	I	N	D	L	E	A	R	W	P	D	T	T	E
T	L	J	T	N	E	L	G	V	A	M	M	V	Q	P	B
B	A	A	S	B	F	B	P	A	S	B	A	Y	J	P	L
A	R	Z	E	S	G	K	Z	S	L	P	R	N	D	B	Z
Y	L	Z	F	Z	X	Z	X	K	K	U	G	K	C	H	Z
L	A	C	I	S	U	M	U	R	V	Z	G	N	L	E	B
Y	P	X	N	O	A	I	T	U	I	B	E	L	V	C	G

SOLUTION ON PAGE 145

PERFORMANCE   ROCK   DOCUMENTARY   JAZZ   MUSICAL
ALBUM   POP   CONCERT   LIVE   FESTIVAL

Dustin Hoffman and Jon Voight in "Midnight Cowboy" Dir. by John Schlesinger (1969)

Social Revolution in Cinema

The "Social Revolution in Cinema" refers to a period when film began to address social, political, and cultural issues in a more direct and frank manner. During the 1960s and 1970s, amidst significant social movements such as civil rights, women's liberation, opposition to the Vietnam War, and the rise of the counterculture, cinema became a vehicle for exploring and questioning established norms.

Filmmakers of this era brought previously taboo subjects such as sexuality, race, war, and political power to the screen. This was manifested in Hollywood and around the world; in France, for example, the Nouvelle Vague challenged conventional cinematic narratives and aesthetics, and in Latin America, cinematography was used as a tool for social resistance and change.

These changes in the film industry also had a direct impact on audiences and censorship policies. Movies began to reflect greater expressive freedom, leading to a liberalization of film rating systems, allowing adult viewers to access more complex and mature content. Films like "Bonnie and Clyde", "Midnight Cowboy", "The Graduate", and "Easy Rider" resonated deeply with a young and changing audience, symbolizing their spirit of rebellion and desire for social change.

This period also marked the beginning of what became known as "New Hollywood" or the "Director's Era," where directors enjoyed greater creative freedom and control over their projects, allowing for a blossoming of innovative styles and narratives.

The "Social Revolution in Cinema" left a significant legacy in the industry. It created space for new voices and perspectives, changed the way stories were told on the screen, and set a precedent for cinema to continue reflecting and driving social change. Cinema became a mirror of tumultuous times, capturing the essence of an era of change and leaving a profound impact on popular culture.

Social Revolution in Cinema

W	J	X	D	Z	C	X	P	G	O	Z	G	V	W	Q
L	Y	P	O	F	K	U	T	N	Q	N	F	Q	Z	U
D	I	C	H	A	N	G	E	O	G	G	T	C	J	G
M	G	Q	T	R	A	W	C	I	V	Q	Z	H	G	N
X	W	S	U	D	Y	K	N	L	V	I	K	E	U	J
P	W	T	O	L	M	T	O	L	L	K	X	G	I	O
Z	A	H	Y	Y	A	O	O	E	S	P	O	A	T	X
R	N	G	S	B	D	Q	V	B	R	P	V	S	F	P
T	Y	I	D	H	E	O	K	E	J	T	L	R	I	S
X	F	R	Z	A	L	S	S	R	M	S	E	Y	N	W
W	R	W	O	L	X	S	T	M	A	E	Q	I	N	U
X	X	B	H	I	I	Y	M	I	D	T	N	M	T	Q
D	Z	Q	D	O	C	Q	N	O	U	O	D	T	G	A
J	Z	A	N	O	Z	Q	M	H	N	R	D	M	G	X
V	M	G	T	Q	S	G	L	P	T	P	P	O	V	F

SOLUTION ON PAGE 145

| REBELLION | PROTEST | CHANGE | EXPRESSION | MOVEMENT |
| FREEDOM | YOUTH | WAR | RIGHTS | LOVE |

Cinema in the Cold War

V	K	V	S	P	T	F	V	I	T	R	V	P	Y
F	D	A	N	I	A	T	R	U	C	L	R	C	Y
J	B	E	P	T	Z	I	M	D	I	K	P	J	U
Z	S	S	F	N	T	H	R	I	L	L	E	R	H
D	P	P	T	E	X	F	B	T	F	G	T	M	K
Z	L	I	Y	G	C	W	G	N	N	V	H	E	H
S	N	O	C	A	J	T	Z	R	O	T	T	D	B
T	O	N	K	E	A	Y	O	E	C	I	V	K	O
G	I	A	M	G	T	Q	I	R	O	N	V	U	N
C	S	G	J	X	J	D	U	I	M	J	C	S	D
Q	N	E	X	H	E	I	C	D	S	Q	M	I	E
R	E	P	O	Y	G	S	Q	D	Y	P	X	Z	J
O	T	Y	F	Y	M	A	R	N	T	M	G	J	G
Z	W	G	A	G	O	T	H	D	P	D	W	M	Y

SOLUTION ON PAGE 145

| ESPIONAGE | BOND | DEFECTOR | AGENT | THRILLER |
| CURTAIN | IRON | CONFLICT | SPY | TENSION |

Francis Ford Coppola directing Marlon Brando in "The Godfather" (1972)

The Godfather

"The Godfather", directed by Francis Ford Coppola and released in 1972, is more than a movie; it's a cultural phenomenon that transformed the gangster film genre and left a lasting impact on cinema history. Adapted from Mario Puzo's eponymous novel, the "Godfather" trilogy chronicles the epic story of the Corleone family, a mafia dynasty embroiled in a struggle to maintain power in a world rife with corruption, betrayal, and violence.

Marlon Brando's portrayal of Vito Corleone, the family patriarch, stands as one of the most memorable performances in cinema history. Brando immersed himself in the character, even altering his physical appearance to more closely resemble a genuine mafia Don. For Marlon Brando's transformation into Vito Corleone in "The Godfather," a dental prosthesis known as a "plumper" was used. Brando initially used it during the screen test to make his character resemble a "bulldog" more. For the film's shooting, a dentist made him a custom-made oral piece to create his sagging cheeks. This prosthesis was designed by legendary makeup artist Dick Smith and manufactured by a New York dentist named Henry Dwork. His first prototype, made of more comfortable foam latex, made Brando's face look too soft and droopy, so they asked for it to be redone in steel and resin.

Brando often improvised on set, which, although initially causing frustration among the production team, eventually enriched the film's authenticity and depth. His portrayal of Vito Corleone, with his whispering voice and imposing presence, became the gold standard for mafia characters in cinema.

The film, divided into a trilogy, is acclaimed for its complex narrative that masterfully blends family drama with political and criminal intrigue. Coppola, with his masterful direction, and cinematographer Gordon Willis, with their innovative use of light and shadow, created an atmosphere that evokes both the grandeur and decay of mafia life.

The influence of "The Godfather" extends beyond its cinematic impact; it has become a staple of popular culture, cited and referenced in countless subsequent works. The trilogy not only elevated Coppola and Brando to legendary status but also established a new paradigm in film storytelling, demonstrating cinema's power to explore the depths of ambition, loyalty, and morality.

The legacy of "The Godfather" endures through generations, not just as a cinematic masterpiece but as an eternal reflection on power and the consequences of our choices. The Corleone saga remains a testament to the art of storytelling at its finest, a saga that continues to fascinate, move, and inspire audiences worldwide.

Major Film Genres of the 1970s & 1980s

```
K R I H O Q U U U Z J L G
S Z O Q O A N Y A G Z M J
R C I R F L U C I U C Y P
X A I A R A X D S O R D J
G H C F X O N X Z J A E B
R E L L I R H T G M K M L
U C Y T B C V A A Q J O O
I N Z Q E V C R F S D C E
C A P A I T D U V L Y V S
L M U S I C A L Z H H H Y
E O J O P R L U R T B Z K
A R N Y R E T S Y M T I G
M Q U G R P H Y P G U C S
```

SOLUTION ON PAGE 146

| COMEDY | ROMANCE | ACTION | MUSICAL | THRILLER |
| DRAMA | MYSTERY | SCIFI | HORROR | FANTASY |

68

Sylvester Stallone in a scene from the first "Rocky" Dir. by John G. Avildsen (1976)

ROCKY BALBOA

The blockbuster era, which began in the 1970s, marked a significant shift in the film industry. With the success of movies like Steven Spielberg's "Jaws" and George Lucas's "Star Wars," film studios realized the potential of big-budget productions to generate massive revenue, leading to a trend of making high-budget movies intended to attract large audiences and generate substantial income.

In this context, "Rocky," written and starring Sylvester Stallone, emerged and was released in 1976. The film, telling the story of an underdog boxer who gets the chance to fight for the heavyweight world championship, was an unexpected triumph both critically and financially, winning three Academy Awards, including Best Picture.

The impact of "Rocky" on the industry was monumental. It not only catapulted Stallone to fame, turning him into one of Hollywood's most recognized faces, but it also demonstrated the potential of inspirational "rags-to-riches" stories to connect with audiences globally. Stallone, who wrote the script in three days, infused the character of Rocky Balboa with a mix of vulnerability and determination that resonated deeply with the audience.

The sequence of the Philadelphia Museum of Art stairs, where Rocky ascends during his training, became a symbol of perseverance and personal triumph. This scene is emblematic not only within the film but also in popular culture, representing the struggle and effort needed to overcome obstacles. The "Rocky Steps" have become a pilgrimage site for fans and a tangible reminder of the film's legacy.

The "Rocky" saga continued with several sequels, each building on the character's legacy and exploring new aspects of his life and career. The franchise not only solidified Stallone's career but also marked a turning point in the sports film genre, inspiring numerous boxing and personal growth films that followed.

"Rocky" also established a formula for future blockbusters, combining personal stories with spectacle, memorable music, and exciting action scenes. The "Rocky" saga remains a benchmark in the industry, highlighting how a well-constructed character and an inspirational narrative can capture the public's imagination and have enduring success across generations.

Blockbuster Era Begins

R	A	Z	C	T	K	A	C	T	N	L	J	D	C	K	C	N
J	I	S	S	E	X	W	F	E	A	S	S	S	A	M	I	S
F	Z	K	P	R	H	A	Z	Z	L	Z	S	W	E	N	B	T
C	X	H	T	M	E	H	J	V	I	V	B	N	C	G	E	T
I	S	S	Z	I	O	D	O	T	E	I	Z	I	M	C	U	U
J	B	R	X	N	W	G	I	E	N	T	C	Q	Z	P	U	R
C	F	H	E	A	G	E	S	A	E	R	G	D	S	W	R	R
B	L	D	O	T	F	V	M	I	R	D	Y	W	T	R	E	Y
C	R	X	T	O	S	R	T	O	C	B	S	R	Q	Z	F	R
I	Z	T	M	R	E	U	Z	N	A	A	K	L	T	T	U	Z
S	S	N	S	P	E	C	B	I	B	N	C	X	L	Y	I	K
S	H	X	U	W	A	G	S	T	A	R	W	A	R	S	E	A
A	D	S	W	A	J	N	J	X	S	K	R	O	S	T	R	E
R	E	A	W	V	Z	C	P	G	Y	O	C	J	W	S	T	W
U	F	B	Y	S	A	P	P	L	A	K	H	E	P	H	M	A
J	D	V	M	H	O	R	Q	Q	Y	B	M	G	P	Q	V	R
F	H	D	J	H	K	V	L	I	Q	Z	Q	K	X	J	Q	Q

SOLUTION ON PAGE 146

SUPERMAN **STARWARS** **ROCKY** **RAIDERS** **GHOSTBUSTERS**
GREASE **JURASSIC** **ALIEN** **JAWS** **TERMINATOR**

STANLEY KUBRICK

Stanley Kubrick, born on July 26, 1928, in New York City, stands as one of the most influential and revered filmmakers of the 20th century. His journey from photography to directing some of the most iconic and groundbreaking films in cinema history is a testament to his genius.

Kubrick's early fascination with chess, photography, and film led him to work as a photographer for "Look" magazine before fully immersing himself in the world of cinema. His debut film, "Fear and Desire" (1953), though self-financed and later dismissed by Kubrick himself, marked the beginning of his illustrious film career.

Kubrick first gained significant attention with "The Killing" (1956), a heist thriller, but it was "Paths of Glory" (1957) that began to cement his reputation as a distinguished director. The film, starring Kirk Douglas, is a biting critique of military bureaucracy and injustice, themes that would recur throughout his work.

In 1960, Kubrick directed "Spartacus," a historical epic that also featured Douglas. Despite production challenges, the film was both a critical and commercial success. However, it was "Dr. Strangelove or: How I Learned to Stop Worrying and Love the Bomb" (1964) that showcased Kubrick's ability to blend satire, black humor, and social commentary amidst the backdrop of the Cold War.

"2001: A Space Odyssey" (1968) set a new standard in the science fiction genre with its innovative special effects, enigmatic narrative, and profound exploration of themes such as human evolution and artificial intelligence. The film is hailed as one of the greatest cinematic masterpieces.

Kubrick continued to delve into various genres with films like "A Clockwork Orange" (1971), a dystopian story based on Anthony Burgess's novel; "Barry Lyndon" (1975), a period drama renowned for its stunning cinematography; "The Shining" (1980), an adaptation of Stephen King's horror novel; "Full Metal Jacket" (1987), a raw depiction of the Vietnam War; and finally "Eyes Wide Shut" (1999), a psychological thriller that explored themes of sexuality and human relationships, which was his last film before his death on March 7, 1999.

Kubrick was known for his perfectionism, meticulous attention to detail, and reclusiveness. He preferred to work away from Hollywood pressures, which allowed him almost total creative control over his projects. Although his approach sometimes led to tensions with actors and collaborators, his legacy as a visionary and pioneer in cinematic art remains deeply respected and celebrated. His work continues to inspire filmmakers and cinephiles for its originality, thematic depth, and innovative techniques.

New Hollywood Directors

A	R	F	L	C	S	N	M	P	Z	G	Y	N	L
Z	G	L	I	H	G	S	Q	E	F	P	U	A	T
I	G	R	E	B	L	E	I	P	S	H	H	M	N
A	Y	W	N	W	U	U	E	P	G	I	F	T	H
L	V	N	C	O	M	C	R	K	V	E	A	L	V
L	K	A	Y	K	K	U	E	S	D	B	P	A	Y
E	C	Y	L	I	I	K	S	N	A	L	O	P	I
N	I	M	N	O	U	O	E	I	E	N	Q	U	J
G	L	P	E	B	P	Y	S	B	Y	K	V	I	R
C	A	U	R	C	Z	P	R	A	B	C	F	B	W
H	M	I	I	Y	F	B	O	B	C	X	A	A	L
W	C	W	L	U	S	R	C	C	H	U	A	M	G
K	C	F	E	S	S	T	S	V	I	K	L	F	Q
U	I	V	N	S	V	D	V	I	U	L	U	K	W

SOLUTION ON PAGE 146

SPIELBERG   POLANSKI   SCORSESE   PECKINPAH   LUCAS
ALTMAN   COPPOLA   KUBRICK   MALICK   ALLEN

MERYL STREEP

Meryl Streep, or Mary Louise Streep, was born on June 22, 1949, in Summit, New Jersey. From her childhood, she demonstrated a natural talent for acting, participating in theatrical productions during her school years. Despite her initial inclination towards law, her true passion for acting led her to change direction and fully commit to the dramatic arts, culminating in a Master of Fine Arts from Yale University.

After graduating, Streep moved to New York, facing the usual challenges for actors at the beginning of their careers. However, her perseverance and dedication quickly bore fruit. She rapidly stood out for her ability to delve into characters and her skill in handling various accents, which allowed her to play a wide range of roles. From her impressive Polish accent in "Sophie's Choice" to her convincing British accent in "The Iron Lady," Streep has shown astonishing versatility that has made her one of the most respected actresses of her generation.

Her career has been marked by a series of memorable performances that have made a significant impact on the film industry. Streep has been recognized with numerous Academy Award nominations, establishing herself as the actress with the most nominations in the history of these awards (21 nominations and 3 awards), a testament to her exceptional talent and dedication to the craft of acting.

Beyond her film career, Streep has also been an active figure in various social and political causes, using her platform to advocate for women's rights, gender equality, and environmental protection, among others. Her commitment to these issues has been as much a part of her legacy as her unforgettable performances.

In summary, Meryl Streep is an extraordinary actress, whose career is characterized by the emotional depth of her interpretations and her unwavering commitment to excellence in her art. Her legacy in cinema is vast, not only for her achievements and recognitions but also for her lasting influence on actors, actresses, and filmmakers alike.

Iconic Actors & Actresses of the 70s & 80s

```
Q G A N D Y U R F R O V P S
L L O N I C A P C S R N A F
B Z V Q R C T S Z D I V W M
L K J F X E H G O E N S Q Z
Z U V T S T V O B K E B G A
F A C M Q M W A L K D F D Z
E G L L Q T M S E S R N C K
F R P T S Z I L J W O V U S
S K E A T O N A E F F N T J
A E E M C T K P M U D Q A E
Y C E V I D O S T R E E P X
U Q O S M B O L F O R D I O
A Y E Y G X K V Y L Q N W K
F R C P D K G L G A T C D J
```

SOLUTION ON PAGE 146

NICHOLSON **EASTWOOD** **PACINO** **REDFORD** **WEAVER**
KEATON **DENIRO** **FONDA** **STREEP** **FORD**

The Master Buñuel. Survivor & Genius

Luis Buñuel, born in Calanda, Teruel, Spain, has established himself as one of the most influential and visionary directors of the 20th century, leaving an indelible legacy in international cinema. His career spans from his early involvement in surrealism in Europe to his consolidation as a filmmaker in Mexico, masterfully addressing social criticism, absurdity, and surrealism.

Buñuel moved to Paris in the 1920s, where he deeply engaged with the surrealist movement alongside figures such as Salvador Dalí. Together, Buñuel and Dalí created "Un Chien Andalou" in 1929, a masterpiece of surrealist cinema that challenged narrative and visual conventions with its famous eye-cutting scene, and "L'Age d'Or" in 1930, known for its bold social criticism and provocative content.

After the Spanish Civil War, Buñuel went into exile in Mexico, where his career flourished with emblematic works that explore the human condition through a critical and surrealistic lens. Among his most notable films from this period is "Los Olvidados" (1950), a harrowing portrayal of disadvantaged youth in Mexico City that earned international recognition at the Cannes Film Festival.

One of Buñuel's pinnacle works is "The Exterminating Angel" (1962), a film that encapsulates his critique of social conventions and the upper class. Through the premise of a group of bourgeois individuals unable to leave a party, Buñuel explores themes of isolation, despair, and the absurd nature of human existence, using surrealism to delve into the collective psyche and expose the fragility of social norms.

Buñuel continued his exploration of religious, moral, and existential themes in films such as "Simon of the Desert" (1965) and "The Discreet Charm of the Bourgeoisie" (1972), the latter winning the Oscar for Best Foreign Language Film, where he satirizes the hypocrisy and emptiness of the upper class with his characteristic wit and surrealistic mastery.

Buñuel's impact on cinema extends beyond his films; his bold approach and rejection of traditional narrative conventions have inspired generations of filmmakers and artists. His work is a testament to the struggle against oppression, the absurdity of existence, and the relentless pursuit of freedom through art.

For a deeper understanding of Luis Buñuel's life and work, it is advisable to explore academic sources and specialized critiques that delve into his filmography, his impact on global cinema, and his contribution to surrealism and social criticism through cinema. It is well worth the investigation, and we invite you to do so.

Influential International Cinema

W	M	V	I	A	W	E	J	Q	J	K	E	X	S	B
K	N	U	L	O	N	F	M	Z	L	C	Q	N	R	W
T	U	A	F	F	U	R	T	V	N	H	U	O	E	X
P	O	K	M	Z	O	Q	N	H	O	X	K	M	D	D
U	J	Y	E	G	W	B	X	C	A	G	G	R	N	S
T	Y	X	C	W	R	T	V	W	E	O	S	E	E	Y
D	W	D	E	O	C	E	A	C	Z	R	Q	D	W	Y
V	M	K	F	H	C	S	B	R	C	S	M	N	J	Z
H	H	X	D	P	O	W	E	O	K	H	M	I	J	S
Q	P	U	T	R	D	H	Z	H	A	O	R	B	A	Z
C	L	E	U	N	U	B	J	M	J	E	V	S	N	O
S	K	K	A	F	M	G	P	E	I	V	J	S	J	C
B	A	Q	R	L	A	S	P	R	N	G	B	A	K	Z
F	S	V	Q	P	F	I	N	I	L	L	E	F	Q	Y
U	A	B	Z	D	U	C	O	N	H	I	P	S	Y	Z

SOLUTION ON PAGE 147

FASSBINDER BERGMAN BUNUEL TARKOVSKY WENDERS
TRUFFAUT HERZOG FELLINI KUROSAWA ROHMER

Michael J. Fox and Christopher Lloyd in the iconic mall parking lot scene (Part I)

Back to the Future. An Iconic Legacy Through Time

"Back to the Future" is not just a film; it's a cultural phenomenon that transcends generations, becoming a foundational pillar in the history of cinema. Released in 1985 and directed by Robert Zemeckis, this cinematic masterpiece propelled Michael J. Fox and Christopher Lloyd into fame, who became the emblematic faces of an adventure that defies the barriers of time.

For those unfamiliar, the plot centers on Marty McFly, an American teenager from the '80s, who accidentally travels 30 years back in time to 1955 in a DeLorean modified by the eccentric scientist Dr. Emmett Lathrop Brown, known to all as Doc Brown, or simply Doc, as Marty calls him. What follows is a thrilling series of events that challenge the space-time continuum, interlaced with humor, drama, and a touch of romance, creating an unforgettable narrative that has captivated audiences of all ages across generations.

One of the most remarkable aspects of "Back to the Future" is its ability to weave together science fiction with comedy and adventure, presenting complex concepts in an accessible and entertaining manner. The film delves into profound themes such as destiny, friendship, and the consequences of our actions, all within the framework of an exhilarating time-travel journey.

The cultural impact of "Back to the Future" is undeniable. It has inspired countless works of fiction, television shows, and has left an indelible mark on pop culture. Phrases like "Great Scott!", "Is anybody home, McFly?", "Nobody calls me chicken," and "Where we're going, we don't need roads," have become part of the popular lexicon, demonstrating the film's timeless resonance.

The soundtrack, composed by Alan Silvestri, along with the hit "The Power of Love" by Huey Lewis and the News, not only captured the essence of the '80s but also became timeless symbols of nostalgia and innovation.

"Back to the Future," completed as a trilogy with its sequels "Back to the Future Part II" (1989) and "Back to the Future Part III" (1990), is not only a technical and narrative achievement but also a testament to vision and passion. The meticulous attention to detail, from the iconic DeLorean to the subtle cultural differences between the decades, demonstrates the production team's commitment to crafting an authentic and immersive cinematic experience.

In conclusion, "Back to the Future" is more than a movie: it is a legacy, a touchstone in cinematic narrative, and a reminder that sometimes, looking back is the best way to understand our present and shape our future. In paying tribute to this cinematic gem, we celebrate not just a work of art but also the power of film to unite, inspire, and transport us to places on journeys we can only dream of.

We highly doubt there's anyone who isn't familiar with it, but for those who have yet to see it, you are delaying the inevitable joy of sitting down to watch and enjoy a unique adventure... Will you be able to watch it just once?

1980s Teen & Family Films

B	Y	Q	X	N	I	Y	X	B	P	G	D	J	T	V	A	Y
S	L	W	S	I	T	C	R	P	M	B	P	O	Z	L	C	J
B	K	I	S	W	N	K	Q	S	N	N	Z	C	M	S	N	K
Q	C	J	B	R	Y	N	I	N	J	Y	L	S	N	I	J	E
W	A	R	M	N	J	Q	H	A	T	J	F	F	Y	T	F	D
N	B	T	H	I	H	E	W	O	D	L	M	Z	S	V	T	E
S	R	E	T	S	U	B	T	S	O	H	G	O	N	O	E	X
L	W	E	E	G	Y	M	R	A	L	D	Z	F	I	D	O	T
S	S	T	T	T	F	V	B	F	R	A	Q	L	L	P	C	S
D	O	S	C	N	L	D	V	F	S	A	L	C	M	K	K	A
T	T	U	V	C	S	E	E	Y	X	E	K	A	E	N	W	F
M	F	Y	C	B	T	R	J	R	D	J	I	K	R	X	S	K
Z	X	S	K	D	R	V	C	U	Q	I	J	N	G	W	R	A
Y	E	C	C	I	Y	F	E	N	I	L	G	J	O	S	E	E
T	C	G	S	O	A	U	S	B	S	C	T	D	T	O	H	R
D	U	E	I	B	F	F	U	T	U	R	E	N	J	H	G	B
E	V	N	K	P	K	A	N	O	W	D	S	N	H	U	W

SOLUTION ON PAGE 147

GREMLINS   BEETLEJUICE   FERRIS   FUTURE   GHOSTBUSTERS
GOONIES   BREAKFAST   ELLIOT   BACK   KARATE

When Monsters & Creatures Came to Life

From the shadows of the earliest cameras to the glow of modern screens, the film industry has witnessed a technological metamorphosis that has revolutionized the way stories are told and experienced.
Cinema, an art form born of the industrial age, has evolved in tandem with technological advancements. With the advent of animatronics, fantastical creatures sprung to life with a verisimilitude that neither pure performance nor traditional animation could match. Skin wrinkles, eyes shift, and a mechanical sigh can send shivers down the spine as authentically as if it emanated from a living being.

The introduction of the IMAX format broadened filmmakers' visions, inviting audiences to immerse themselves in images of unprecedented scale and clarity. Meanwhile, advancements in sound, particularly those developed by Dolby, have refined the capture and reproduction of audio, from the subtlest whispers to the loudest explosions, enveloping viewers in an auditory tapestry as rich as the world around them.

Chroma key, often simply referred to as green screen, has been the invisible brush with which directors have painted universes beyond the confines of our reality. This technique has been a cornerstone in the creation of visual effects, allowing artists and technicians to meld actors into any environment imaginable, from futuristic cities to distant planets.

Digitalization has touched every stage of film production. Digital capture, non-linear editing, and projection have simplified and democratized the filmmaking process, enabling content creators at all levels to partake in cinematic storytelling.

The Steadicam, as an extension of the filmmaker's hand, has allowed the essence of human movement to be captured without sacrificing the smoothness of the image. Through a carefully choreographed dance between operator and camera, shots that are poetry in motion are achieved.
In the realm of animation, we've seen an evolution from painstaking hand-drawings to the computer-generated marvels that fill today's screens. Digital animation has brought to life worlds and characters with a detail and complexity that defy the imagination.

Finally, stereoscopic cinema has transcended mere visual gimmickry to become a narrative tool that, when used skillfully, can deepen the emotional connection and presence within the film's world.

These advancements are not just tools; they are extensions of the cinematic language that have opened new horizons for visual storytellers. Each new technology has enabled filmmakers to take audiences on richer, more immersive journeys, challenging and delighting our senses. In paying homage to these innovations in our book, we celebrate not just the technical prowess behind the films we love, but also humanity's relentless quest for magic and wonder, and how, through cinema, we transform light and sound into palpable emotions and enduring memories.

Advances in Film Technology

N	F	K	K	M	X	F	A	C	O	Q	A	F	L	N	E	F
G	L	N	C	A	J	V	W	F	Y	M	Y	I	Q	H	G	V
N	E	M	C	C	M	D	A	W	D	Y	N	Q	F	F	H	L
G	H	N	Z	I	T	Z	P	P	B	L	K	Y	X	N	H	N
L	G	M	B	D	P	I	F	M	K	U	A	W	A	R	Z	H
J	O	M	W	A	Q	O	T	B	A	O	N	T	M	X	X	Y
E	W	H	Q	E	T	I	C	W	G	N	I	T	I	D	E	B
F	N	B	I	T	E	Q	P	S	K	L	M	E	T	G	O	L
H	B	R	G	S	O	X	T	L	O	I	A	T	V	P	I	O
H	C	H	R	O	M	A	K	E	Y	E	T	P	K	F	K	D
J	M	T	F	K	U	O	E	R	D	K	R	F	R	P	F	Q
C	G	O	Z	S	Q	Y	B	G	S	N	O	E	L	A	F	W
R	H	I	L	D	Q	Z	S	Y	U	H	N	K	T	D	H	W
T	T	B	R	B	N	O	I	T	A	M	I	N	A	S	Y	C
U	N	Q	A	T	F	U	V	J	E	F	C	O	O	O	K	H
K	D	B	S	W	L	W	O	N	B	S	S	D	R	E	T	P
J	G	S	O	W	Y	D	O	S	R	K	B	X	P	U	G	V

SOLUTION ON PAGE 147

ANIMATRONICS DIGITAL STEREOSCOPIC CHROMAKEY DOLBY
ANIMATION SOUND STEADICAM EDITING IMAX

Spike Lee directing one of the scenes from "Do the Right Thing" (1989)

The Indie Movement

The independent cinema of the 1980s marked a decisive turning point in the history of film. This period was characterized by a creative effervescence that challenged the conventions of the industry and provided a platform for alternative voices and innovative narratives.

During the '80s, indie cinema benefited from a confluence of social and technological factors. On one hand, the counterculture of the preceding decades had sown a desire for personal and artistic expression that found no place in the mainstream cinema dominated by Hollywood's major studios. On the other hand, the advent of accessible technologies, such as video cameras and Super 8 film, allowed independent filmmakers to produce their works with reduced budgets.

Distribution and exhibition also underwent significant changes. Film festivals, like the Sundance Film Festival—founded in 1978 as the Utah/US Film Festival—became essential meeting points for independent filmmakers, where they could showcase their works and find distribution. Moreover, the rise of video rental stores and the proliferation of VHS gave independent films a new channel to reach audiences.

Directors such as Jim Jarmusch with "Stranger Than Paradise" (1984), the Coen brothers with "Blood Simple" (1984), and Spike Lee with "She's Gotta Have It" (1986) or "Do The Right Thing" (1989) burst onto the scene with distinctive styles and fresh narrative approaches. Their films not only found success among critics and audiences but also inspired a new generation of filmmakers to take the independent route.

Indie cinema of the '80s was also characterized by exploring themes often ignored or superficially treated by more commercial cinema, such as diversity, identity, sexuality, and social critique. These films had the freedom to be more experimental, both in content and form, moving away from traditional narrative and aesthetic formulas.

In summary, the indie movement of the '80s proved to be a laboratory of ideas and styles that not only enriched cinematic language but also paved the way for auteur cinema to establish itself more strongly in the global industry. These filmmakers left an indelible mark, establishing a legacy that continues to influence contemporary cinema.

Cult Films & Movements

```
F M K O O Y F X K E Y G N E D F Z
E V Y B L P A K P P F N T S W G P
R X E T W Q N J Z B J E C U H D I
P O L X E U Z C H M G T G O C L N
W O P N P O U A I A I E G H H A W
M J G X V L N M X U B D U D P Q N
X W E D T D O P Z G X S N N J A U
A C U E O I A I K R L H G I H R E
M B W S C L Z M T F V R M R G T Z
W K J Z J T K L D A K I X G M H Y
A S Q S R I J R R X T L K K Q O T
J G D K D Y I Q Z F I O K K U R
I R I R B U N G T Q S P O V V S P
K P T Y M D O V I C D W L N A E J
N E A C I R I F M Y U B I X P U Y
V F N E E Z R S B F P U R U Y Y M
Q K Z Z U L Q G B C O L P L Q U L
```

SOLUTION ON PAGE 147

| EXPLOITATION | PUNK | GORE | CAMP | ARTHOUSE |
| GRINDHOUSE | INDIE | NOIR | CULT | MIDNIGHT |

Documentary & Realism

K	X	M	P	X	M	T	O	G	T	Y	R	V	O
E	E	W	B	K	J	T	G	J	C	N	R	B	L
P	S	A	F	Z	K	H	K	V	A	G	H	P	E
C	O	Z	Q	H	P	E	L	T	E	S	L	T	E
D	P	L	D	U	O	E	U	I	F	R	U	V	Z
C	X	K	I	F	W	R	S	R	K	V	I	V	F
S	E	W	S	T	E	S	X	O	T	H	R	T	O
S	R	B	N	B	I	O	P	I	C	C	A	W	E
P	K	Z	W	P	V	C	I	R	K	I	B	W	E
T	L	U	H	F	R	X	A	J	X	N	A	S	J
D	R	P	R	A	E	O	M	L	G	L	F	L	Y
I	S	R	T	T	T	T	R	N	L	X	H	Y	G
R	O	M	S	I	N	G	Y	C	X	D	Z	C	Q
K	M	Q	W	O	I	C	M	D	U	Y	V	N	A

SOLUTION ON PAGE 148

| INTERVIEW | NATURE | VERITE | WALL | ARCHIVE |
| POLITICAL | EXPOSE | BIOPIC | FLY | SOCIAL |

Christopher Reeve in one of the iconic scenes from "Superman" Dir. by Richard Donner (1978)

Superman (1978)

The 1978 film "Superman," directed by Richard Donner and starring Christopher Reeve, is a cinematic landmark that not only revitalized the superhero genre but also set a standard for comic book adaptations on screen.

The production of "Superman" was a bold gamble by producers Alexander and Ilya Salkind, who foresaw the potential of superheroes on the big screen long before it became the norm. The film pioneered a serious approach to the source material, in contrast to the lighter, campier adaptation of 1966's "Batman." The Salkinds were visionary in simultaneously producing the first two Superman films, an ambitious strategy underscoring their confidence in the project.

Initially, the direction of the film was offered to Richard Lester, who declined because the project didn't align with his style and he wasn't very familiar with Superman. Guy Hamilton was then considered for direction, but due to legal issues with Marlon Brando related to his film "Last Tango in Paris" (1972), they couldn't shoot in Italy as initially planned, shifting production to England. Hamilton, being a tax exile, couldn't stay in England for more than thirty consecutive days, ultimately leading to Richard Donner's selection as director after the producers were impressed with his work on "The Omen" (1976).

The search for the ideal actor to play Superman was extensive, initially considering several stars like Paul Newman, Sylvester Stallone, and Robert Redford. However, Donner insisted that Superman should be portrayed by an unknown face to the audience, ultimately leading to the choice of Christopher Reeve. Reeve underwent intense physical training under the supervision of David Prowse (who played Darth Vader) to build the necessary physique for the role.

Donner was unsatisfied with Guy Hamilton's special effects proposals and relied on John Barry to define the aesthetics of Krypton and Smallville. For the flying scenes, numerous techniques were tested until an innovative solution combining the use of wires and trampolines with pre-recorded backgrounds was found, achieving a convincing flight effect.

"Superman" was nominated for 3 Academy Awards in the categories of Best Editing (Stuart Baird and Michael Ellis), Best Original Score (John Williams), and Best Sound (Gordon K. McCallum, Graham V. Hartstone, Nicolas Le Messurier, Roy Charman). Additionally, it received a Special Achievement Award for Visual Effects from the Academy in the same year.

The 1978 film "Superman" is much more than a comic book adaptation; it is a cinematic masterpiece that combines memorable performances, innovative special effects, and skilled direction to create an unforgettable experience. It is a testament to the talent and vision of its creators and a reminder that at the heart of the best superhero stories lies the ability to make us believe in the impossible. The film not only made us believe that a man could fly; it taught us the value of hope, justice, and humanity.

Rise of Action Heroes & Superheroes

```
C T X E H P O C O B O R M D P
D O O E M P R U U I B R R V L
T Y P M F H P J S G N A A R G
H I N W S Y N V E Q N M O P L
B S P G Z Q N A M T A B I W I
N B P V W S Q T M P Y O J J G
T E R M I N A T O R I G G S B
A N O Y H F Z S P E E M A T W
S A E X V J R K L D T P L R K
A L I Y L I N D I A N A U U A
Z C C B V B F B M T V B I S U
A C R L W O O V M O V S Y X Z
Y M H S B F Q R N R O H S I J
S N N G Q S L N I X Z F G Y Y
G T K H B O N D S P X O U C B
```

SOLUTION ON PAGE 148

TERMINATOR   **PREDATOR**   **SUPERMAN**   **RIGGS**   **BATMAN**
ROBOCOP   **MCCLANE**   **INDIANA**   **BOND**   **RAMBO**

DID YOU KNOW?...

Blade Runner
- Ridley Scott originally considered Dustin Hoffman for the lead role before choosing Harrison Ford.
- The famous tear in Rutger Hauer's eyes at the end of the film was improvised by the actor.

Metropolis
- It's said that actress Brigitte Helm, who played Maria, sustained injuries during filming due to the difficulty of some scenes, such as the flooding in the underground city.
- Fritz Lang hired hundreds of extras for the scene of the workers in the underground city, many of whom were real unemployed people from Berlin living in poverty.

Alien
- The scene where the alien slides out of the egg was filmed using a combination of real animal organs and seafood to create an authentic organic appearance.
- The design of the spaceship Nostromo was partly inspired by the work of Swiss artist H.R. Giger, whose biomechanical creations shaped the film's unique visual aesthetic.

2001: A Space Odyssey
- To create the weightlessness effect in the spaceship sequences, Stanley Kubrick employed a technique known as "human gyroscope," where actors were suspended by harnesses and filmed while spinning in a revolving room.
- The famous transition sequence where a bone transforms into a spaceship was originally conceived as a transition between the Stone Age and the Space Age, symbolizing human progress throughout history.

Tron
- The visual effects of Tron, innovative for its time, were heavily inspired by 1980s video games.
- To achieve the film's unique visual look, actors wore white and black suits and were lit with neon lights on a dark set.

Dune
- The original Dune film from 1984 had an elaborate marketing plan that included the release of a comic book and the production of toys, but the film's box office failure led to the cancellation of these plans.
- David Lynch, the director of Dune, later admitted he was not familiar with Frank Herbert's novel when he agreed to direct the film and only read it once before starting production.

Akira
- The movie Akira was originally intended to be an adaptation of the entire manga series, but due to time and budget constraints, only a portion of the story was adapted.
- Akira pioneered the use of "limited animation" technique, where only key elements of a scene are animated to save time and resources.

Mad Max
- Before becoming an actor, Mel Gibson worked as an employee in a candy factory.
- The film was shot on real locations in Australia during the summer, resulting in extremely hot and challenging conditions for the cast and crew.

RoboCop
- Peter Weller, who played RoboCop, spent months working with a mime coach to learn how to move robotically and express emotions through the robot suit.
- During the filming of RoboCop, actor Kurtwood Smith, who played the villain Clarence Boddicker, often improvised his lines, contributing to the intensity and authenticity of his performance.

Solaris
- Andrei Tarkovsky, the director of Solaris, insisted on filming the movie on natural locations instead of using special effects, adding a sense of authenticity and depth to the film.
- Tarkovsky filmed many long, static shots in Solaris to encourage contemplation and reflection in the viewer, contributing to the film's slow-paced and meditative rhythm.

Landmark Science Fiction Films

W	Y	P	J	M	T	Z	M	L	S	B	P	O	I	Z	B
B	F	H	V	M	C	J	I	X	O	E	N	J	E	V	I
U	L	D	U	K	T	W	E	O	T	E	X	B	C	Z	A
N	N	A	X	K	M	I	E	H	N	G	M	L	A	Z	P
O	Q	G	D	Z	E	V	W	Z	Q	R	Q	C	O	Z	K
R	I	U	A	E	T	O	T	Z	W	R	S	M	J	O	E
T	N	J	S	O	R	C	M	S	T	R	O	T	E	E	A
E	R	S	P	T	O	U	Y	V	Q	K	L	A	A	P	U
Z	M	F	A	G	P	J	N	X	J	Z	A	A	B	H	A
V	P	H	S	O	O	T	A	N	U	J	R	P	D	P	Y
H	R	X	C	N	L	C	M	O	E	O	I	O	J	U	R
B	H	F	G	F	I	Z	P	A	B	R	S	U	N	A	B
Q	V	W	V	F	S	C	Q	O	D	Y	S	S	E	Y	L
C	B	G	B	T	T	P	C	N	S	M	N	V	I	T	K
J	F	T	V	A	O	O	A	K	I	R	A	N	L	C	T
S	W	S	Q	N	P	L	J	B	K	L	B	X	A	J	X

SOLUTION ON PAGE 148

| BLADERUNNER | ALIEN | ROBOCOP | MADMAX | AKIRA |
| METROPOLIS | DUNE | SOLARIS | ODYSSEY | TRON |

Bill Murray

Bill Murray, born on September 21, 1950, in Evanston, Illinois, is an esteemed American actor and comedian, celebrated for his deadpan delivery across a spectrum of roles, from mainstream comedies to indie dramas. His career trajectory took off with "The National Lampoon Radio Hour," leading to national recognition on "Saturday Night Live" from 1977 to 1980, where he clinched a Primetime Emmy Award for Outstanding Writing for a Variety Series. Murray secured his celebrity status through a succession of hit comedies such as "Meatballs" (1979), "Caddyshack" (1980), "Stripes" (1981), "Ghostbusters" (1984), and "Groundhog Day" (1993), and also embraced supporting roles in movies like "Tootsie" (1982) and "Little Shop of Horrors" (1986). His directorial venture is marked by "Quick Change" (1990).

Murray's frequent collaborations with directors like Wes Anderson and Sofia Coppola have been pivotal, featuring in multiple Anderson films including "Rushmore" (1998), "The Royal Tenenbaums" (2001), "The Life Aquatic with Steve Zissou" (2004), and "The Grand Budapest Hotel" (2014), as well as Coppola's "Lost in Translation" (2003). His performance in the latter won him Golden Globe and BAFTA Awards, alongside an Academy Award nomination for Best Actor. His role in the HBO miniseries "Olive Kitteridge" (2014) earned him his second Primetime Emmy Award.

Raised in an Irish Catholic family as one of nine children, Murray's early life was shaped by his work as a golf caddie to fund his Jesuit high school education. He briefly joined a rock band called The Dutch Masters and was involved in high school and community theater. After high school, he attended Regis University in Denver, Colorado, but soon dropped out and returned to Illinois. A pivotal moment in his life occurred when he was arrested at Chicago's O'Hare Airport for attempting to smuggle cannabis, leading to his conviction and probation.

Murray's unique personality and fan interactions have made him a beloved figure both in and out of the film industry. His contributions to television and film, combined with his distinctive humor and depth of character, have established him as a comedy icon and a respected actor in more dramatic roles

Comedy Icons of the 70s & 80s

V	T	F	T	U	H	G	W	T	O	H	J
L	D	D	O	W	C	C	R	B	P	S	B
M	C	O	I	H	L	A	V	L	U	F	Z
A	O	H	Y	L	V	I	R	L	N	A	C
R	T	I	A	D	H	Y	I	L	Y	H	Y
T	E	T	A	S	N	E	A	H	I	S	H
I	S	D	U	U	E	A	N	R	T	N	P
N	W	L	L	T	X	M	C	O	R	Y	R
W	E	N	X	I	K	F	F	Y	L	U	U
B	M	T	R	K	W	D	A	R	N	B	M
W	A	Y	K	R	O	Y	D	P	K	L	U
H	C	Y	K	Z	B	L	U	Z	Y	M	R

SOLUTION ON PAGE 148

| AYKROYD | WILDER | MURPHY | CARLIN | MURRAY |
| BELUSHI | PRYOR | MARTIN | CHASE | CANDY |

89

Kathryn Bigelow

Kathryn Bigelow is a prominent American filmmaker, born on November 27, 1951, in San Carlos, California. She is renowned for her adeptness at directing action films often featuring protagonists grappling with internal conflicts. Bigelow holds the distinction of being the first woman to win an Academy Award for Best Director for "The Hurt Locker" in 2008, a film that provides an intense, personal look at modern warfare.

Prior to her film career, Bigelow dedicated herself to painting, studying at the San Francisco Art Institute and participating in the Independent Study Program at the Whitney Museum of American Art in New York. Her early interest in visual arts is evident in her cinematic approach, where she often experiments with form and narrative style.

Bigelow made her directorial debut with "The Loveless" in 1981 and continued to break molds with films like "Near Dark" (1987), which blends Western and vampire genres. In 1990, "Blue Steel" offered a fresh perspective on action films, followed by the iconic "Point Break" (1991), which, despite mixed reviews, achieved box office success and a cult following.

Throughout her career, she has explored complex and often controversial themes, as seen in "Strange Days" (1995), addressing issues such as racism and abuse of power. After a five-year hiatus from directing, she returned with "K-19: The Widowmaker" (2002) and then achieved critical and commercial success with "The Hurt Locker" (2008), followed by "Zero Dark Thirty" (2012), focusing on the hunt for Osama bin Laden, and most recently "Detroit" (2017), examining the 1967 Detroit riots.

In addition to her big-screen achievements, Bigelow has also worked in television, directing episodes of series and winning a Primetime Emmy Award for Exceptional Merit in Documentary Filmmaking for "Cartel Land" (2015). Her work often challenges expectations and genre conventions, and she continues to be an influential and respected voice in the film industry.

Influential Female Directors

```
E R U V I L O X K S O J Y K R C
X P U C K N N A C X A I Q W R J
V D H I H K B O B E R W D P M K
U X F N M L P U Q L I V E V V V
U G I Z N P L V D J U A G F W Z
E O D F O N C Y A M M R B E C C
L C N L I O G F N R L S R C O T
M W A H P P Z B L I D T J K R M
G P L R M M A K E R M A N B U U
S K L Y A N R E V U D H Q I N T
E A O H C V F J L M X H R G P P
E Y H M J F K L Q D C J L E E J
C O R I E F E N S T A H L L Q D
H B K M G R L N J B T Y Z O D Y
B U Y B L A P O T A Q Z P W Q Z
O D T X Z T W O A T D S F F X X
```

SOLUTION ON PAGE 149

WERTMÜLLER COPPOLA VARDA HOLLAND DUVERNAY
RIEFENSTAHL CAMPION MAY BIGELOW AKERMAN

Buzz Lightyear and Woody in a frame from "Toy Story," Dir. by John Lasseter (1995)

Breakthrough in Animation & Special Effects

In the late '80s and early '90s, the realm of animation and special effects encountered a transformative era that would forever reshape its future. During this pivotal time, animation giants like Disney embarked on what would be known as the Disney Renaissance, crafting films that not only revived the genre but also became timeless classics. Traditional animation, with its meticulous attention to detail and fluidity of motion, reached new heights with films such as "The Little Mermaid" and "The Lion King," captivating audiences of all ages.

Simultaneously, a burgeoning studio named Pixar was charting its revolutionary course. With the release of "Toy Story," Pixar didn't just prove that fully digital animation was possible, but it could also weave stories with heart and depth, setting new standards for visual storytelling and animation technology.

Meanwhile, in Japan, Studio Ghibli, under the direction of maestros like Hayao Miyazaki, was crafting cinematic artworks that stood out for their complex narratives and beautiful animation. Films like "My Neighbor Totoro" and "Princess Mononoke" not only solidified anime's standing in the world but also took the medium in new artistic directions.

Claymation, with its tactile charm and capacity to breathe life into imaginative worlds, continued to captivate audiences with films like "The Nightmare Before Christmas," showcasing the ability to tell dark and complex stories through this form of stop-motion.

Anime, with its range of styles and genres, gained international acclaim during this period, challenging Western expectations about animation and broadening its reach to a more mature audience with titles like "Akira," a film that remains influential for its style and cultural impact.

Technically, rotoscoping, though not new, was refined to create more fluid and lifelike movements, while early experiments in motion capture began to hint at a future where the lines between live-action and animation would blur.

Digitization would become the next great leap, facilitating not only the creation and manipulation of images but also changing the workflow of traditional animation and allowing for visual effects that were previously impossible or prohibitively expensive to achieve.

This period of innovation and experimentation not only expanded the boundaries of what animation could achieve but also set the stage for decades of advancements to come, heralding a new era where animation and special effects would become an integral part of cinematic storytelling, opening a world of limitless possibilities for story-telling.

Breakthrough in Animation & Special Effects

```
T B I I P F M D C I J D R R K
U Y Y G I X G W N G W V W X N
Q Q B A S A Y S V G W I F E T
G F E C T F A A I B U R R G Y
L H P K Q B N S Q Z A U K D E
V A I Q C R K P X M T H G V N
Z U M B X P A V E P H R B Z S
N C D C L A Y M A T I O N H I
D U U F L I P C T I X T M V D
V L A T I G I D S R Q O J S S
Y M M I O F X Q Q E T S C W X
O U U I R X A Z T I E C B R D
A H R G S R R H O J D O P O R
M A R K K D W N B M L P W Y J
Y H E M I N A X O R I E X Z A
```

SOLUTION ON PAGE 149

| CLAYMATION | CAPTURE | DISNEY | GHIBLI | DIGITAL |
| ROTOSCOPE | MOTION | PIXAR | ANIME | FRAME |

CHAPTER THREE
1990-2023

Quentin Tarantino. The Rebel of Modern Cinema

Quentin Tarantino is one of the most influential and recognized film directors of recent decades. Born on March 27, 1963, in Knoxville, Tennessee, Tarantino grew up as an avid cinephile. His distinctive style, characterized by witty dialogue, stylized violence, and cinematic references, has made him an icon of contemporary cinema.

His love for cinema ignited during his formative years, while working at a video rental store where he engaged in enriching conversations about film, a period that significantly contributed to his vast knowledge and passion for cinema. Tarantino's career as a director took off in the early 1990s, marking the beginning of a revolutionary chapter in film history. His unique approach to storytelling and characterization quickly distinguished him as a creative force to be reckoned with in the entertainment industry.

His first feature film, "Reservoir Dogs" (1992), was acclaimed by critics and established his reputation as an innovative director. However, it was his second film, "Pulp Fiction" (1994), that catapulted him to international stardom. "Pulp Fiction" was a box office hit and won the Palme d'Or at the Cannes Film Festival, in addition to receiving multiple awards and nominations, including seven Academy Awards.

Tarantino is known to be extremely meticulous in every aspect of his film projects, from selecting music to choosing set props. Famous for carefully curating the music in his works, he often resurrects forgotten or lesser-known songs that become hits after he has used them.

He treasures an impressive collection of films in 35 mm format and is known for his passion for analog cinema. It is said that he has an extensive personal film library spanning a wide range of genres and eras, and he often hosts private screenings for his friends and colleagues at his own home.

The revolutionary success of "Reservoir Dogs" and "Pulp Fiction" heralded the advent of a transformative era in the resplendent tapestry of contemporary popular culture, a fervent testimony to the indomitable and resounding genius that would come to define the unwavering charm of the modern cinema master. With each resonant and evocative work, Tarantino further solidified his status as a preeminent figure in the pantheon of cinema virtuosos; his indomitable spirit and unwavering and resounding creativity continue to resonate in the hallowed halls of cinematic adulation and resounding acclaim from audiences and industry alike.

In summary, Quentin Tarantino is a visionary filmmaker whose impact on the film industry is undeniable. His unique style and bold approach have left an indelible mark on contemporary cinematic culture, and his legacy will continue to resonate with future generations of cinephiles and filmmakers.

Cinema in the 1990s

O	L	A	W	M	D	S	U	E	C	X	U	Q	R	R	E	Y
G	B	R	M	T	O	S	D	J	E	O	X	Q	H	H	L	D
S	C	X	L	W	W	C	N	P	A	W	J	S	O	K	E	I
L	O	N	L	T	L	V	K	F	P	P	E	U	L	Y	Q	N
P	M	A	T	R	I	X	N	U	Y	J	A	B	F	V	H	D
M	L	Q	C	V	U	T	W	H	M	E	B	E	S	M	I	I
C	M	G	Q	I	T	F	A	R	Y	E	S	Y	N	G	G	E
M	M	X	W	M	K	Z	D	N	X	T	N	E	I	I	B	I
J	Z	O	Z	X	Z	Q	A	N	I	M	A	T	I	O	N	S
T	X	W	B	H	P	X	S	V	L	C	A	A	A	T	P	K
M	O	S	I	N	I	I	A	V	T	L	F	R	E	R	W	R
B	M	W	O	N	T	L	M	P	Z	Q	K	A	T	O	Y	G
G	Z	I	P	S	B	X	Y	K	Y	D	U	N	I	P	O	D
H	W	P	I	V	Y	D	U	Z	X	O	I	T	D	R	V	Q
V	G	Q	C	R	T	Q	U	F	Q	I	V	I	O	F	Z	U
O	R	K	X	W	A	N	I	M	E	S	S	N	I	H	C	V
N	S	C	I	I	W	Y	N	J	M	F	K	O	P	Y	U	L

SOLUTION ON PAGE 149

TARANTINO MOCKUMENTARY DIGITAL MATRIX TITANIC
FESTIVAL ANIMATION INDIE ANIME BIOPIC

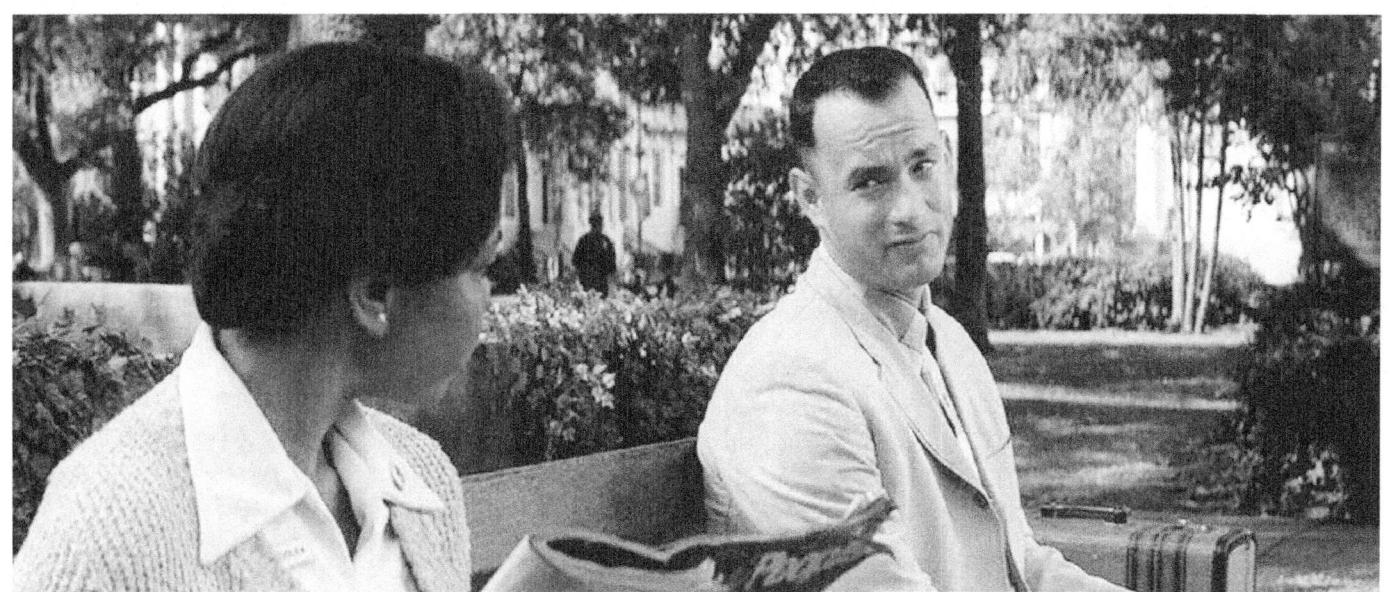

Tom Hanks and Margo Moorer in the iconic bench scene from "Forrest Gump" Dir. Robert Zemeckis (1994)

Forrest Gump: Heart, Comedy & History

"Forrest Gump," a 1994 film directed by Robert Zemeckis and based on the novel of the same name by Winston Groom. This movie is known for its unique and emotive narrative, as well as for the outstanding performances, especially that of Tom Hanks in the lead role.

It is considered an iconic film that left an indelible mark on popular culture and the history of cinema. It won several major awards, including six Academy Awards, including Best Picture and Best Actor for Tom Hanks. It masterfully combines elements of comedy, drama, history, and romance, making it a unique work that has been studied and analyzed by cinephiles and academics.

Tom Hanks's portrayal of Forrest Gump is one of the most memorable performances of his career. Before Tom Hanks was chosen to play Forrest, the role was offered to John Travolta, who turned it down. This rejection turned out to be a blessing for Hanks, who managed to capture the innocence, kindness, and complexity of the character in a way that resonated deeply with audiences. His dedication to the role was evident in his performance, and his ability to convey Forrest Gump's emotions earned him the Academy Award for Best Actor for the second consecutive year after winning it the previous year for "Philadelphia" directed by Jonathan Demme in 1993.

Innovative techniques were used to integrate Forrest Gump into archival footage of historical events. This allowed the character to interact with historical figures such as John F. Kennedy, Richard Nixon, and John Lennon, creating memorable and convincing moments on screen. Additionally, visual effects were used to create some of the most stunning scenes, such as when Forrest runs through a battlefield in Vietnam.

The iconic scene where Forrest runs across the United States on foot took several months to film. Tom Hanks and the production team traveled to various locations across the country to capture the sequence, with Hanks actually running long distances.

Another curiosity of the film is that when Gump meets his son for the first time, the child playing Forrest's son is actually Tom Hanks's real-life son, Colin Hanks, in his film debut.

Tom Hanks waived his usual salary for "Forrest Gump" in exchange for a percentage of the film's profits. This decision turned out to be extremely lucrative, as the movie was a major box office success and one of the biggest hits of his career.

"Forrest Gump" became a cultural phenomenon in the 1990s and remains a beloved film worldwide. Its iconic lines, such as "Life is like a box of chocolates, you never know what you're gonna get," "Lieutenant Dan! Lieutenant Dan!", "Stupid is as stupid does," or "Run Forrest!! Run!!," have become part of the popular lexicon. The film also addressed important themes such as war, disability, and love, making it a profoundly moving and relevant masterpiece.

Influential Films of the 1990s

```
N U J I O O B H V J W P H P
Z X C L U E L E S S H L D A
D Y B X I L W A O M I O H S
C V L Q S O D T A G R V M I
I X T J B B N A M U R T B G
J L V U L U F K K C D A Y O
A H S R F L L O I X M D F Z
S L L A K C D A R N C E M Z
I H P S H T D K M R G A W N
X Z E S C H I N D L E R J P
B J E I X G Y V X R S S W X
Z U I C F I C R C V K P T P
Q B Q T V F Z S D R T F K O
R N B H Q I U M X E D O G R
```

SOLUTION ON PAGE 149

| FIGHTCLUB | SCHINDLER | TRUMAN | CLUELESS | FARGO |
| LIONKING | JURASSIC | FORREST | SCREAM | HEAT |

Pixar Animation Studios

"Pixar Animation Studios is the crown jewel of the animation film industry and has woven a tale of innovation, creativity, and unprecedented success since its inception. The story of Pixar dates back to 1979 when it began as part of Lucasfilm's computer graphics division, named The Graphics Group. This seedling of innovation blossomed in 1986 when Steve Jobs, co-founder of Apple, saw its potential and acquired the company, renaming it Pixar. With an investment of $5 million from Jobs for its purchase and an additional $5 million in operating capital, Pixar began its journey, marked by initial financial challenges but driven by an unwavering vision towards innovation in computer animation.

The partnership with Disney for film production and distribution was a turning point. "Toy Story" (1995), Pixar's first feature film, marked a before and after in animation, being the first movie entirely animated by computer. This milestone was not only a technical achievement but also showcased the power of emotional narratives and endearing characters, establishing Pixar as a leader in the field. This initial success laid the groundwork for a series of innovative films that combined heartwarming stories with technological advancements, such as "Monsters, Inc.", "Finding Nemo", "The Incredibles", and "WALL-E", each pushing the limits of what was possible in digital animation.

The merger of Pixar with The Walt Disney Company in 2006 for $7.4 billion was a reflection of its invaluable status within the industry and cemented its position as a titan in animation. Under the creative leadership of figures like John Lasseter and Ed Catmull, Pixar maintained its ethos of innovation and narrative quality, even as it expanded within the Disney conglomerate.

Pixar has not only been a pioneer in animation techniques and storytelling but has also significantly influenced popular culture and the film industry. Its films often explore deep themes such as identity, loss, friendship, and family, making them relevant to audiences of all ages. Additionally, the company has been a leader in animation technology, developing software like RenderMan, which has been used in the production of numerous films inside and outside of Pixar, winning technical Academy Awards for its contribution to the film industry.

Its impact extends beyond its cinematic and technical achievements. The company has set a new standard in the animation industry, demonstrating that animated films can be as rich and complex in narrative and characters as any live-action film. Moreover, it has inspired generations of animators, artists, and filmmakers to dream big and push the boundaries of their creativity.

Pixar's influence on the film industry is a testament to its unique approach to filmmaking, where the story reigns supreme, and technology serves to bring those stories to life in more vivid and emotionally engaging ways. Through its journey, Pixar has maintained a balance between art and technology, advancing the medium of animation while touching the hearts of millions worldwide, securing its place in film history as a true innovator and storyteller.

Rise of Animation Studios

```
P C K N D M S W V N X J C B J H L
L M H H R S P G S G S R K Q U T N
W H S Q Q C B M X V T Z K O Y L O
X M V D R L M R J T A Y F Z K T I
J D K B T Q F S N H K H H T H Y T
W H L D N T I Y S F G K Y Z E A
B I V M O A P E E R I V J S R R N
U L U D N I M U X E C F D O M O I
Z F O G X L L D I S N E Y S E W M
L R N A M B D D R V S T H D W P U
J L R P H I D R E A M W O R K S L
N L O I D H L A I K A L E B O Y L
R L C V V G M G U K E I H N Q J I
H L L C Q N X V W K H H Y Z B R Z
H T K N T T X J C B Z Q S J V X N
F L U V N F O I T P R P N D S P V
C V I C V D N D I O T P Q M S B N
```

SOLUTION ON PAGE 150

NICKELODEON   ILLUMINATION   DISNEY   BLUESKY   LAIKA
DREAMWORKS   AARDMAN   PIXAR   GHIBLI   SONY

Major Film Genres of the 90s & 2000s

```
O G O J S L U X R G Q R A G
N A W F T S Z M N Q M W D M
T H R I L L E R U N Y R R C
B J A S B B A D U R Z R B B
J K Y B U N D R I S G Z H V
F J R W O P V J F H B Y S O
J P E I I E E A M Q R C U J
B U T I B K N R V Q I Z G R
W C S L H T T X H F L O S P
A Y Y N A O U Z I E D V W X
J K M S K J R O L B R G B Z
R S Y S S C E R E L T O A Y
M V W N D H D M O C M O R C
V E S Z R B N K D R A M A C
```

SOLUTION ON PAGE 150

| ADVENTURE | MYSTERY | THRILLER | ROMCOM | DRAMA |
| SUPERHERO | HORROR | FANTASY | ACTION | SCIFI |

101

Wes Anderson. A Parallel Universe

Wes Anderson, the mastermind behind the quirky, has woven a unique tapestry in the history of cinema through his filmography. Born in Houston, Texas, on May 1, 1969, Anderson discovered his love for cinema at an early age, captivated by the power of movies to construct their own worlds. His academic background at the University of Texas at Austin, where he met Owen Wilson, his future collaborator, became the breeding ground where his artistic vision began to germinate.

Anderson's career took off with "Bottle Rocket" (1996), a crime comedy that, although not a box office hit, captured the attention of critics and established the foundation of his style: eccentric characters, sharp dialogues, and meticulously cared-for aesthetics. "Rushmore" (1998) and "The Royal Tenenbaums" (2001) cemented his reputation, the latter earning him an Oscar nomination for Best Original Screenplay.

Anderson's filmography is characterized by its distinctive focus on visual symmetry, pastel color palettes, and detailed storytelling, elements that have become his signature. Movies like "The Life Aquatic with Steve Zissou" (2004) and "The Grand Budapest Hotel" (2014), for which he won the Golden Globe for Best Motion Picture – Musical or Comedy, demonstrate his ability to merge the comedic with the melancholic, creating universes that, although they may seem detached from reality, reflect the complexities of the human condition.

Anderson has frequently collaborated with a set of actors, including Bill Murray, Tilda Swinton, and Jason Schwartzman, creating a sort of repertory company that has enriched the cohesion and emotional depth of his work. His foray into animation with "Fantastic Mr. Fox" (2009) and "Isle of Dogs" (2018) expanded his creative reach, demonstrating that his unique aesthetics and narrative transcend the medium.

Wes Anderson's meticulousness and perfectionism in composing each scene are well-known in the cinematic world. His almost artisanal approach to the creation of detailed filmic universes is manifested in his use of detailed models, a practice that underscores his commitment to a distinctive and coherent visual aesthetic.

These models, miniature replicas of his film settings, not only serve as previsualization tools but also reflect the importance of symmetry and precision in his work. Through them, Anderson can experiment with the arrangement of elements, from decorative objects to the placement of characters, ensuring that each component of the scene contributes to the visual narrative in a meaningful way.

This method allows Anderson and his production team to anticipate challenges and optimize the filming process, ensuring that the artistic vision remains intact throughout the production. By meticulously visualizing and adjusting every detail in these models, Wes Anderson ensures that the final composition on screen captures the essence of his unique style, where every element, no matter how small, plays a crucial role in the storytelling.

Anderson's dedication to this level of detail not only enriches the visual experience for the audience but also sets a standard for art direction in contemporary cinema, demonstrating how precision in preproduction can translate into a visually cohesive and aesthetically innovative masterpiece.

In summary, Wes Anderson is not just a director; he is a storyteller whose vision and way of doing things have left a personal and unique style in the cinematic landscape. Through his lens, the ordinary is transformed into the extraordinary, making each film a work of art worthy of being explored again and again.

2000s New Wave & Indie Directors

U	Y	A	V	D	Z	S	W	G	W	J	K	M	I
O	U	M	D	S	E	Y	Q	Z	S	L	B	W	P
B	G	A	B	Z	G	L	R	K	C	V	R	E	W
R	E	B	R	E	I	R	T	N	O	V	D	H	O
E	W	U	E	O	X	B	E	O	U	Q	M	E	N
H	Y	C	T	H	N	H	A	T	R	A	Q	K	G
Q	S	Y	A	I	V	O	W	T	A	O	E	V	A
I	C	Q	L	K	R	W	F	M	F	J	U	M	A
V	S	O	K	A	S	R	M	S	K	P	U	Z	T
Y	O	H	N	O	O	J	A	Z	K	B	B	E	E
Z	F	U	I	P	F	C	R	N	F	Y	W	B	M
T	J	Q	L	G	I	D	R	F	I	S	J	K	P
D	X	R	J	Q	A	W	O	W	V	I	C	X	T
N	O	L	A	N	O	S	R	E	D	N	A	T	P

SOLUTION ON PAGE 150

ARONOFSKY   ANDERSON   VONTRIER   DELTORO   GRETA
LINKLATER   INARRITU   JOONHO   NOLAN   SOFIA

Raj Malhotra and Simran Singh in a still from "Dilwale Dulhania Le Jayenge" Dir. by Aditya Chopra (1995)

Bollywood. Bringing Cultures Together Through Dance

Bollywood, the film industry based in Bombay, India, is one of the largest and most prolific in the world, known for its vibrant musicals, emotive stories, and a unique fusion of tradition and modernity. Over the years, Bollywood has had a significant influence on global cinema, marking its presence not only in South Asia but in various parts of the world.

The term "Bollywood" is a portmanteau of Bombay (the former name of Mumbai) and Hollywood. Though it primarily refers to the Hindi-language film industry, it is often used more broadly to describe all Indian cinema. The first wholly Indian film, "Raja Harishchandra," was a black-and-white silent feature produced and directed by Dadasaheb Phalke in 1913. This film is considered the beginning of the Indian film industry.

During the 1940s and 1950s, Indian cinema experienced its "Golden Age," with films addressing the social and political issues of the time, many of which received international acclaim. Legendary figures like Raj Kapoor, Guru Dutt, and actress Nargis, among others, contributed to the flourishing of Bollywood during these years.

Bollywood is famous for its elaborate dance and music sequences. Music is an essential component of its films, to the extent that India's music industry is intrinsically linked to cinema. Playback singers, who record songs for actors to lip-sync on screen, are celebrated figures in India, with Lata Mangeshkar and Kishore Kumar being two of the most iconic.

In recent decades, Bollywood has gained an international audience, with films being screened worldwide and festivals dedicated exclusively to Indian cinema. The rise of the Indian diaspora has played a crucial role in this phenomenon, leading to an increase in the demand for Bollywood films outside India. Moreover, globalization has facilitated greater exposure and accessibility through digital platforms and social media, allowing Bollywood to influence and be influenced by other film industries.

Contemporary figures like Shah Rukh Khan, Aamir Khan, and Priyanka Chopra have significantly contributed to Bollywood's global recognition. Films like "Lagaan," "Dangal," and "Slumdog Millionaire" (though the latter is a British production, it is deeply rooted in Bollywood's culture and aesthetics) have received international attention, participating in prestigious film festivals and being nominated for Academy Awards.

Bollywood's impact on world cinema is also evident in how it has inspired international filmmakers and fostered cross-border collaborations. The industry continues to evolve, addressing contemporary issues and experimenting with new genres and narrative formats, while still maintaining the traditions that make it unique.

Bollywood is not just the heart of Indian cinema but a cultural force that continues to leave its mark on the global cinematic landscape, celebrating the richness and diversity of India's stories and traditions, while engaging with audiences and filmmakers around the world.

Global Cinema in the New Millennium

```
F A Z J F C T S A V M Y M R
Y E V P T M L H J D D B I K
N A C I X E M N H U Z B E C
H I D E W L I C Z A R J Q U
S D Z J S F N B Y A F I O Q
J A P A N E S E Z N L R N Y
T Z T A R O N I Q P N A A O
P G C F G B L I Q S L N E L
K T M S N I A L H R G I R C
D W P L A K S U Y C Z A O A
H R I N Z O M V I W V N K K
Q C N A I S S U R Z O Z S D
T S E O D O O W Y L L O B G
N O L W O M D S D L C D D G
```

SOLUTION ON PAGE 150

| NOLLYWOOD | BRAZILIAN | RUSSIAN | CHINESE | MEXICAN |
| BOLLYWOOD | JAPANESE | FRENCH | KOREAN | IRANIAN |

105

Audrey Tautou in a still from "Amelie" Dir. by Jean-Pierre Jeunet (2001)

Amelie. A Love Letter to Parisian Magic

"Amélie," directed by Jean-Pierre Jeunet in 2001, is a contemporary cinematic gem that captures the essence of Parisian charm through the eyes of its protagonist, Amélie Poulain. The film is an ode to the beauty of everyday life, enveloped in a whimsical aura that sets it apart in the cinematic landscape.

The story centers on Amélie, masterfully portrayed by Audrey Tautou, a young waitress who decides to improve the lives of those around her while grappling with her own solitude and longing for connection. What makes "Amélie" unique is not just its plot, but how Jeunet weaves a visual and narrative tapestry that transforms the mundane into the magical. The cinematography, rich in saturated colors, and meticulous art direction, create an idealized Paris that is as much a protagonist as Amélie herself.

A variety of creative techniques and approaches were employed during filming to capture the film's unique essence. It's interesting to note how Jeunet achieved the distinctive visual style of the film, characterized by its vibrant shades of green and red. This was accomplished not only through art direction and location selection but also through the use of digital post-production processes to enhance these colors.

The soundtrack, composed by Yann Tiersen, is another key element that adds a layer of charm to the film. The unmistakably Parisian accordion and piano melodies evoke a sense of nostalgia and joy that reinforce the film's whimsical tone. Songs like "La Valse d'Amélie" not only complement the narrative but have become synonymous with the film, leaving an indelible mark on popular culture.

"Amélie" is also notable for its focus on life's small pleasures and the importance of human connections. Through Amélie's interventions in the lives of others, Jeunet invites us to reflect on the impact that acts of kindness can have in an often indifferent world. The film reminds us of the magic of small moments and the beauty found in simplicity.

Thematically, "Amélie" explores loneliness, love, childhood, and the pursuit of happiness in a world that sometimes seems devoid of it. Amélie herself is an unusual heroine; her shyness and vivid imagination make her a character with whom many can identify, and her journey towards self-discovery and fulfillment is both moving and inspiring.

The café where Amélie works, the "Café des Deux Moulins," is a real establishment located in Montmartre, Paris. Since the film's release, it has become a pilgrimage site for fans wishing to experience a small part of Amélie's world. However, the café had to be considerably modified for filming, as the real interior was too small and did not match the director's aesthetic vision.

This wonderful 20th-century tale is a masterpiece that celebrates life through the extraordinary in the ordinary. With its unique aesthetic, endearing characters, and memorable soundtrack, "Amélie" has earned a place in the hearts of cinephiles worldwide, becoming a modern classic that continues to enchant and inspire new generations of viewers.

Influential 2000s Films

```
E C D V L D Q X P M Y W Z X J
L O B B O F U T B N B E Z O E
B K T R C I T Y O F G O D D X
Z B H N O O F E I L E M A C L
H G G P E K S E P P Z Z X O U
O X I M Y M E L E S U H J M I
L M N Z C J E B A V A T A R N
D I K K J C B M A D Q N P F Q
B B K N O I T P E C N I W Y E
O L R T A C W T F H K R L H F
Y C A C N D I K M M R Y X C L
A K D W B R M Y P S B B U T K
Q O U E I P L F I N C A D L A
E H R P D P O B H V A L P D O
W X S R B I S V N V T P T A Y
```

SOLUTION ON PAGE 151

DARKKNIGHT   BROKEBACK   INCEPTION   OLDBOY   SPIRITED
CITYOFGOD   LABYRINTH   MEMENTO   AVATAR   AMELIE

Shrek. An Ogre & a Donkey That Enchanted the World

"Shrek," released in 2001, stormed the world of animation with a whirlwind of innovation, humor, and cultural critique. This DreamWorks Animation gem not only cemented digital animation (CGI) as the new gold standard for animated films but also redefined what a film of this genre could be and achieve.

From the start, "Shrek" dared to be different. Instead of sparkling castles and damsels in distress, it gave us a swamp and a grumpy ogre as the protagonist. Shrek, with his grumpy attitude and heart of gold, became the most beloved anti-hero in animation. Accompanied by the charismatic and talkative Donkey, unforgettably voiced by Eddie Murphy, the film turned the typical fairy tale narrative on its head.

"Shrek's" CGI technique was innovative not only for its quality and detail but also because it allowed creators to bring a fantasy world to life with unprecedented realism and expressiveness. This technological approach, coupled with a smart script that blended humor for both adults and children, established a new paradigm in animation cinema. The film demonstrated that CGI animation could be used not only to create fantastical worlds but also to tell complex and emotionally resonant stories.

The "Shrek" soundtrack, with iconic themes like "All Star" by Smash Mouth and Leonard Cohen's "Hallelujah" performed by John Cale, became an important part of the film's identity, adding an extra layer of irreverence and charm. The music played a crucial role in setting the film's cheerful and sometimes bittersweet tone.

But beyond technique and humor, "Shrek" dared to challenge norms and parody the conventions of Disney fairy tales and other classics, presenting themes of acceptance, self-love, and the beauty of imperfection. The relationship between Shrek and Fiona, a princess who defies all stereotypes, is a testament to the film's message that true beauty lies within.

The cultural impact of "Shrek" was enormous, spawning sequels, spin-offs, and a legion of fans who still celebrate its originality and humor today. The film was not only a box office success but also won the first Oscar for Best Animated Feature, securing its place in cinematic history.

"Shrek" was not just a film; it was a phenomenon that forever changed the animation landscape. With its bold humor, technical innovation, and emotional warmth, "Shrek" proved that animated films can be smart, funny, and moving, capable of capturing the hearts of audiences of all ages.

Modern Animation & CGI Advances

```
I  U  U  F  C  F  D  E  L  L  A  W  T
T  F  P  U  M  V  R  V  V  Q  O  G  Z
D  F  A  U  N  J  G  O  B  P  W  Z  S
M  U  C  P  B  S  E  K  Z  D  R  B  D
M  J  O  A  S  D  S  H  R  E  K  J  D
C  R  M  I  H  D  N  T  N  L  N  O  L
N  G  I  P  D  M  O  I  E  G  G  V  Z
U  U  B  O  R  Z  L  R  I  N  Z  X  W
Y  Y  S  T  B  A  D  Q  A  A  K  V  U
P  J  S  O  R  U  E  R  H  T  B  X  J
S  S  G  O  V  E  K  J  Z  A  I  Q  X
U  H  C  Z  A  K  T  H  I  A  I  N  J
F  Z  J  O  M  R  N  Y  X  Q  E  O  T
```

SOLUTION ON PAGE 151

CORALINE **ZOOTOPIA** **MOCAP** **RANGO** **KUBO**
TANGLED **FROZEN** **SHREK** **WALLE** **UP**

Michael Moore

Document to Transform

The 2000s marked a renaissance in documentary cinema, with works that not only captured the public's imagination but also influenced public debate and policy. Michael Moore, with his provocative and confrontational style, led this wave with films like "Bowling for Columbine," which not only challenged viewers to reconsider their viewpoints but also earned him an Oscar for Best Documentary, and "Fahrenheit 9/11," taking the genre to new levels of popularity and relevance.

However, Moore was not alone in this endeavor. Morgan Spurlock, with his immersive and personal "Super Size Me," raised serious questions about the food industry and health, shifting the conversation about fast food. This documentary highlighted the risks of the standard American diet and led to significant changes in how fast-food chains presented their menus.

Alongside them, filmmakers like Errol Morris and Alex Gibney contributed their unique voices to the genre. Morris, with "The Fog of War" (2003), an intense exploration of the 20th-century conflicts through the eyes of former U.S. Secretary of Defense Robert S. McNamara, offered a critical and profound look at the nature of war and power. Gibney, in "Enron: The Smartest Guys in the Room" (2005), exposed the corruption and greed that led to Enron's downfall, providing a scathing critique of unbridled capitalism.

These documentaries and their creators transformed non-fiction cinema into a vibrant platform for exploring complex and urgent topics, from politics and the economy to health and the environment. They did so not only by informing and educating but also by entertaining, using the power of cinema to attract and retain the public's attention.

With their rich diversity of voices and perspectives, the 2000s demonstrated that documentaries could be as dynamic and captivating as any fictional film. The filmmakers of this era not only documented the world around them but also questioned it and, in many cases, fought to change it. Their films are not just witnesses to their time; they are catalysts for reflection and action, demonstrating the power of cinema to illuminate, inspire, and ultimately transform.

Documentary Films & Realism

```
T  H  R  P  Z  P  B  S  Y  K  P  M  V  U  X
C  P  S  U  I  R  X  T  Q  I  C  U  R  Y  U
M  W  M  I  S  R  I  P  V  J  V  L  Q  B  Q
R  J  A  C  F  I  X  N  Q  E  I  T  M  F  K
D  K  E  T  C  K  X  X  G  V  C  R  N  C  I
B  P  R  E  H  N  C  T  N  A  S  L  O  A  C
M  A  D  G  K  L  Y  A  I  G  S  J  N  O  I
L  X  P  F  D  J  O  I  L  X  P  L  J  C  Y
R  X  O  H  S  B  W  N  W  B  E  P  A  H  A
V  E  O  O  K  B  N  R  O  W  O  M  R  N  U
N  D  H  C  N  W  M  G  B  K  P  C  M  B  D
P  E  G  B  F  Y  L  Z  Z  I  R  G  N  O  Y
B  U  E  B  B  O  F  L  Z  M  Z  R  O  G  Z
D  X  F  F  A  R  E  N  H  E  I  T  N  V  D
U  O  H  V  G  G  K  I  T  G  X  Q  T  N  F
```

SOLUTION ON PAGE 151

| HOOPDREAMS | ANVIL | FARENHEIT | EXIT | BOWLING |
| BLACKFISH | ACT | GASLAND | JIRO | GRIZZLY |

111

Rise of Streaming Services

V	O	C	Y	L	U	C	X	E	Z	S	W	B	F	X	Z
X	S	P	S	B	T	Q	I	Y	V	P	U	H	N	X	T
B	Y	S	U	L	U	H	L	W	E	V	O	J	V	S	X
Q	I	I	V	Y	W	J	F	M	P	N	J	T	R	W	H
M	G	E	Y	P	I	Y	T	F	K	K	S	I	C	V	E
D	B	T	T	N	Z	G	E	K	C	C	H	I	S	C	Y
S	O	N	C	R	Q	J	N	O	Z	A	M	A	D	U	D
W	Y	U	G	K	Z	R	P	M	U	N	M	B	T	T	I
L	L	O	R	Y	H	C	N	U	R	C	F	Z	W	V	P
E	M	M	U	C	L	Y	E	B	Q	G	P	T	O	T	L
S	W	A	E	T	P	E	A	C	O	C	K	Q	R	X	C
I	O	R	T	N	U	N	W	B	H	T	A	R	E	G	L
N	P	A	S	U	W	B	H	B	P	Y	G	L	B	T	B
V	B	P	V	E	O	B	E	X	D	Z	P	D	B	P	C
R	Y	B	F	Y	R	H	D	A	I	P	Z	J	R	E	Z
U	E	W	M	M	X	C	X	K	A	I	O	Q	O	A	Q

SOLUTION ON PAGE 151

CRUNCHYROLL   HULU   YOUTUBE   DISNEY   PEACOCK
PARAMOUNT   HBO   AMAZON   APPLE   NETFLIX

21st Century Film Technology

J	O	I	V	K	N	B	R	G	Y	R	D	O	B	R	Z	M
A	S	O	N	Q	D	W	S	F	T	Z	H	E	E	Z	X	S
H	T	F	O	R	P	O	G	P	Q	C	D	D	U	I	H	E
A	E	Z	O	N	Q	C	W	G	I	I	J	O	X	J	M	U
X	R	N	D	E	T	N	E	M	G	U	A	Q	S	Z	Q	M
H	E	W	H	D	O	V	A	I	C	C	C	O	C	Y	E	J
U	O	G	H	A	H	N	T	L	E	X	T	R	Q	N	R	Z
Y	S	M	T	K	Y	A	A	A	C	E	P	G	A	K	Y	O
N	C	M	M	D	L	F	R	U	J	C	X	F	W	C	Z	H
I	O	S	H	F	P	W	O	T	N	P	A	V	L	O	C	P
S	P	G	N	S	C	J	F	R	L	G	X	L	Q	R	X	R
W	I	E	R	W	C	L	X	I	I	U	A	B	T	C	O	O
H	C	V	I	D	K	L	I	V	R	E	M	S	M	Q	X	K
P	K	L	P	Z	X	E	L	T	H	X	I	C	J	X	W	I
J	G	D	B	F	L	E	V	X	Z	L	W	J	K	N	J	J
O	E	L	V	E	Z	V	F	J	F	B	S	D	R	U	S	F
K	O	H	M	D	J	E	F	C	X	T	C	S	K	W	P	M

SOLUTION ON PAGE 152

| HIGHDYNAMIC | AUGMENTED | VIRTUAL | GOPRO | DIGITAL |
| STEREOSCOPIC | ULTRAHD | ATMOS | IMAX | DRONE |

New Genres & Trends

```
G U N K T R I L T E Q P M L G S G
P D Q Y E V D R Y X G Y E E Y Q H
W L Y E S L W D P C I G N E U F R
A D Z R E O H B K N E K A M E R H
R O O O I G O Y I X G N G M H E G
J H W S R U A B P O H R H E O E M
O O Y E E M D T B E P A S F C D M
Q D K F S E J O O R R I A D I K M
Y M C Q B N Z P L O H L C F J L U
Z X W U E T E W D C F W I V N D X
L G O S W A W L N E I D X N G M Y
B U P M A R F A L L V I N I K F F
Y J C J D Y R T O B Z S I U E N J
X M F A N F I L M M Q W I Y O Y O
G I W C M O C K B U S T E R B F V
O N P X Z N K B I M Y L Z B B Q E
V U J T B O R R Y L B Q D M R D X
```

SOLUTION ON PAGE 152

FOUNDFOOTAGE   **HYPERLINK**   **MUMBLECORE**   **FRANCHISE**   **REMAKE**
VLOGUMENTARY   **WEBSERIES**   **MOCKBUSTER**   **FANFILM**   **BIOPIC**

Greta Gerwig, Lynne Ramsay, Sofia Coppola, Lila Avilés, Elisa Miller

Influential Women in Modern Cinema

The modern era of cinema has witnessed the increasing recognition and influence of female directors, who have brought bold narratives and captivating visuals to the big screen. These filmmakers have not only defied expectations with their diversity of voices and unique perspectives but have also inspired future generations in the film industry. They have made a difference with stories that have deeply resonated with audiences and critics, opening new avenues for female creative expression.

Directors like Kathryn Bigelow and Greta Gerwig have broken barriers, the former being the only woman to win an Oscar for Best Direction for a long period, and the latter offering a fresh and authentic perspective in acclaimed films such as "Lady Bird" and "Little Women." Chloé Zhao, with her unique vision and commitment to intimate and immersive narratives, has received recognition and awards, including an Oscar for "Nomadland." Ava DuVernay has used her platform not only to tell powerful stories but also to promote inclusion and diversity in cinema.

Sofia Coppola, known for her distinctive visual aesthetic and focus on themes of femininity, has created worlds that are both visually enchanting and narratively rich, while Patty Jenkins has reinvented the superhero genre with "Wonder Woman," showing that big-budget films can also have female direction.

These directors have carried out films that transcend genres, from intimate dramas to action blockbusters, illustrating that women in direction have the capacity to tell any kind of story. They have faced challenges and overcome obstacles, leaving a legacy that not only affects the film industry but also changes the way the public perceives stories and those who tell them.

As we move forward, these women are setting a precedent for a more egalitarian and inclusive cinema, where female directors are celebrated for their art and not limited by their gender. The influence of women in modern cinema continues to be a testament to the power of cinema to evolve and adapt, reflecting the changing dynamics of our society and promoting a culture of equality on and off the screen.

Influential Women in Modern Cinema

O	N	I	K	O	B	F	D	E	J	V	U	Q	A	G
A	B	G	P	W	K	R	U	A	B	S	K	W	F	Y
H	V	V	F	A	C	N	V	J	W	B	E	J	Y	Y
Z	M	Y	N	Z	D	B	E	W	A	I	Y	Z	C	T
O	P	F	Q	A	P	N	R	D	F	G	R	L	B	P
Z	G	J	S	I	K	R	N	K	O	E	C	R	Y	Q
Z	A	Y	Q	I	Z	Q	A	G	P	L	G	N	L	R
N	H	L	N	B	Y	H	M	S	O	O	P	B	T
T	W	S	O	H	P	N	O	G	S	W	N	H	A	H
F	P	F	X	P	S	W	U	E	Q	A	M	N	C	N
E	J	S	M	P	P	O	F	R	K	O	Y	V	Q	S
T	X	U	Z	C	Q	O	Q	W	Q	E	H	Z	I	K
N	S	R	O	O	F	S	C	I	A	M	M	A	B	E
R	X	L	D	E	N	I	S	G	W	D	Q	L	Z	V
X	N	M	K	A	V	K	P	T	W	P	D	C	A	O

SOLUTION ON PAGE 152

CHOLODENKO	**JENKINS**	**BIGELOW**	**SCIAMMA**	**DENIS**
DUVERNAY	**GERWIG**	**RAMSAY**	**COPPOLA**	**ZHAO**

Modern Science Fiction & Fantasy

```
R M L O M W W K T R Y K G I J B X
R A R M E H D W B T N R A R W L Z
R Q L E V X E H C G O F V S E E Y
M T F L P M M I R R I U Z N B T H
R D U N E O R A C X T V W C R I W
E C T Q M T O Y C N A K A W I D V
J Z G X S P S L B H L R W T D A A
A E I I O H Q R Y Q I K T I P M F
D F D F Z N Y I E A H N R G X P T
Z A G C Q A F T N T I Q A R I H J
X L A V I R R A I Z N D G L U J C
C Z U C R E V I Q V N I X I S A P
U L N B H Y W R R S A O S P X F R
T X L O V J E O H F S R O Y F Y K
L C Z V R O R Y F R Q N G M N F S
D K P Q A U C I I T Q Q H R C N K
R O V C I F Y V V Y R B F P Q S T K
```

SOLUTION ON PAGE 152

ANNIHILATION   EXMACHINA   ARRIVAL   DUNE   DISTRICT
INTERSTELLAR   GRAVITY   MOON   HER   LOOPER

Robert Redford, founder of the Sundance Film Festival in 1981

Independent Cinema Evolution

The evolution of independent cinema is a captivating journey from early visionaries like Oscar Micheaux, who sought to tell stories beyond the constraints of major studios, to the digital era that has democratized filmmaking, providing a platform for diverse voices and innovative narratives. Independent films, known for their lower budgets and creative freedom, offer a refreshing alternative to mainstream cinema, allowing filmmakers to explore unconventional subjects and blend various genres.

From John Cassavetes in the United States, recognized as one of the first true independent filmmakers, to Quentin Tarantino, Richard Linklater, and Kevin Smith in the 1990s, these "Indie Auteurs" challenged traditional narratives and introduced new perspectives. "Pulp Fiction" by Tarantino and "Clerks" by Smith became exemplary indie successes, proving that independent films could achieve both critical acclaim and commercial success.

The role of film festivals like Sundance has been crucial in elevating the status of independent films, providing a much-needed platform for filmmakers to showcase their work and for films to gain recognition and commercial success. The Sundance Film Festival, founded by Robert Redford in 1981, became a game-changer by offering indie filmmakers an opportunity to reach a wider audience and secure distribution deals.

In the digital era, independent filmmaking has undergone a significant shift, with more accessible tools and resources to create high-quality films on a limited budget. Streaming platforms like Netflix and Amazon Prime Video have become vital for indie filmmakers, offering a global audience and breaking down traditional film distribution barriers. This has led to a new way of consuming media, with unique viewing experiences increasingly in demand, and filmmakers exploring "hybrid" distribution models that combine different release strategies.

As technology progresses, independent cinema may continue to delve into immersive storytelling through virtual reality, augmented reality, and 360-degree filmmaking, further expanding possibilities for filmmakers. Streaming services have become crucial for indie film distribution, allowing unique stories and perspectives to reach a wider audience than ever before. With a continuous push towards original storytelling and breaking away from mainstream conventions, the future of independent filmmaking looks promising, holding the potential for even more growth and success in the coming years.

For a perfect and faithful translation to American English of the original Spanish text you provided, it would be best to work with a professional translator who can ensure the nuances and subtleties of the language are preserved.

Independent Cinema Evolution

```
R Q B S A W Y I K W E A Q K
E X R D M K S O J B B A F M
L E X N O E N H D E I D N I
E H S J R A W E A I Q W A R
V F B U T N K T I K N J R A
T C A L N Q D A L W Q U T M
I L F Q U D T G Z E S O I A
Q G H I J M A S W U K S S X
E T A I J S H N C B D E A J
N C X N D U V O C A K F N Q
P I E M K T F I U E D D S Z
D I F W N H U L T S M F E I
P F Z W K H U Y K E E P D A
V A M A G N O L I A D R H P
```

SOLUTION ON PAGE 153

| BLUMHOUSE | TROMA | MIRAMAX | NEON | LIONSGATE |
| SUNDANCE | FOCUS | ARTISAN | INDIE | MAGNOLIA |

Avatar. James Cameron's Life Project

James Cameron's "Avatar" is a film that set a new precedent in the film industry due to its technical and narrative innovation. Released in 2009, "Avatar" not only captured the global audience's imagination with its lush world of Pandora and its Na'vi inhabitants but also set new standards for visual effects technology and 3D cinematography. Cameron utilized and enhanced motion capture technology to create the Na'vi characters, allowing for an unprecedented level of facial and bodily expression in CGI characters.

This was achieved by capturing the actors' performances in a studio environment and then rendering those performances onto the digital characters, preserving the subtleties and emotions of the live performances. Cameron and his team developed specific 3D stereoscopic cameras for "Avatar," known as the Fusion cameras. These cameras allowed for high-quality image capture that, combined with advanced rendering techniques, created an immersive and realistic 3D experience.

The creation of the world of Pandora involved the development of detailed and complex virtual environments, posing a significant challenge in terms of rendering and animation. The team used cutting-edge software to model, texture, and light these digital landscapes, creating a rich and convincing alien ecosystem.

The idea for "Avatar" was conceived by Cameron in the early '90s, but he had to wait over a decade for the technology to catch up with his vision. This long gestation period allowed Cameron to immerse himself deeply in the world of Pandora, developing its story, culture, flora, and fauna with an astonishing level of detail.

Cameron didn't just create a visually stunning world; he also developed a complete language for its Na'vi inhabitants, working with linguist Dr. Paul Frommer to create a language with its own grammatical structure, vocabulary, and phonetics. This added a layer of authenticity and depth to the universe of "Avatar."

The production of the "Avatar" sequels has been a lengthy process, with Cameron and his team dedicating years to developing the technology needed to carry out his vision for the subsequent parts. Cameron has promised to explore Pandora further, including its oceans and other regions, which has required even more innovations in motion capture technology and visual effects. "Avatar" and its sequels represent the culmination of James Cameron's passion for exploration and technological innovation.

The film is not only an achievement in terms of narrative and visual effects but has also influenced how films are made and experienced, pushing the boundaries of what's possible in cinema.

Global Box Office Hits

T	R	A	N	S	F	O	R	M	E	R	S	R	Y	P	I	Q
A	Q	F	V	G	T	M	N	J	J	X	K	L	J	R	J	M
F	F	Q	M	A	A	O	E	E	M	B	L	K	D	B	I	G
F	U	G	X	L	T	K	Z	J	Z	L	L	W	M	C	S	S
G	T	Q	L	I	L	A	O	M	M	Z	Z	R	T	Z	B	I
S	M	C	Z	D	Y	A	R	W	P	M	G	A	W	O	T	K
N	D	I	P	I	P	N	F	D	K	T	D	W	B	G	I	T
P	F	A	N	O	Z	D	Y	Y	I	Z	O	N	I	V	L	D
X	C	E	B	I	M	N	X	T	K	E	K	E	N	O	Y	Q
R	Q	A	Z	V	O	I	A	I	H	S	K	G	C	Q	R	L
P	A	N	N	U	G	N	E	N	D	G	A	M	E	V	D	I
Y	G	P	V	E	I	X	S	J	O	Q	I	R	P	R	L	U
E	J	U	L	C	M	W	M	K	U	O	V	L	T	J	V	W
Z	N	R	J	Q	R	Y	L	A	W	K	T	A	I	A	X	V
R	N	Z	B	T	R	Z	M	K	D	O	D	X	O	W	I	X
G	T	S	I	K	C	A	G	U	V	F	K	M	N	M	T	F
M	G	Y	D	Q	N	X	L	I	X	F	W	K	U	M	U	C

SOLUTION ON PAGE 153

TRANSFORMERS AQUAMAN TWILIGHT SKYFALL TITANIC
INCEPTION ENDGAME MINIONS FROZEN AVATAR

Trends in 21st Century Storytelling

```
R T A Q R G N D O L P U D Y C
E E E K Y I A R L H E B X X L
E I B P R G U E C J Y Z G N M
E S Z O A R U P X A X E O U P
Q B R S O Q N K L D F L Q P I
C H B E E T I M E A F I Q N B
V Y E R V J S N U P O U Y T C
F G P Z I I P X Q T N C I R G
Z G D O T J N T E A I L O W Q
D X I R A U X U S T P S G N E
M U C N R B T P Q I S U T C G
S H W E R Y G O L O H T N A J
V X T H A C N L V N V K U J T
H L W V N W X E J P A N E Q H
U V G V K P R U P N Z L B Q G
```

SOLUTION ON PAGE 153

| ADAPTATION | NARRATIVE | PREQUEL | CROSSOVER | SEQUEL |
| ANTHOLOGY | UNIVERSE | REBOOT | SPINOFF | SAGA |

Master John Williams Conducting the Orchestra

Modern Film Soundtracks & Scores

The soul of cinema is often whispered in the melodies and crescendos of its soundtrack. Great composers of original film scores are the unsung architects of emotional resonance, imbuing scenes with a life force that transcends the screen. Names like Hans Zimmer, Alexandre Desplat, Michael Giacchino, Howard Shore, Danny Elfman, John Powell, James Newton Howard, and the legendary Ennio Morricone echo through the annals of film history for their unparalleled talent in weaving narrative and emotion through music. These maestros have crafted the backdrop to cinematic masterpieces, enveloping audiences in a spectrum of feelings, and have been instrumental in setting the tone for some of the most iconic moments in film.

Yet, amidst these titans of the score, John Williams stands as a colossus. With a prolific career that boasts five Academy Awards and an astounding 53 nominations, Williams has bestowed upon the world some of the most recognizable and beloved soundtracks in cinematic history. From the thrilling adventure of "Indiana Jones," the awe-inspiring wonder of "E.T.," to the majestic vastness of "Star Wars," and the soaring heroics of "Superman," Williams's compositions have not only accompanied our collective dreams but have also etched themselves into our cultural consciousness.

The reverberations of Williams's impact, which began with an Emmy-winning score for the television adaptation of "Heidi," are undeniable. He has not only raised the bar for the quality and complexity of film music but has also set a golden standard for how scores can serve the story and stand alone as works of art. His music is timeless and universal, crossing cultural and geographical boundaries to touch the very core of the human experience.

Each of these composers has uniquely contributed to the art of filmmaking. They demonstrate that a well-crafted score can transform a film, elevating every scene to something not only seen but deeply felt. As cinema continues to evolve, the need for composers who can capture the essence of a story through music remains as vital as ever. The original score is not merely an accompaniment; it is a powerful voice in the narrative of our beloved tales.

Modern Film Soundtracks & Scores

D	R	T	D	L	M	H	N	F	U	W	L	A	A
W	H	P	P	L	C	G	O	H	I	V	K	N	E
Q	P	O	Q	G	Q	M	D	Z	N	V	W	P	U
T	N	W	N	Z	L	Z	V	A	E	G	H	J	D
A	V	E	E	I	M	J	M	N	I	C	Y	E	C
B	V	L	R	M	H	F	O	T	V	I	S	L	X
S	E	L	O	M	L	C	J	S	E	P	F	O	A
D	P	J	H	E	I	X	C	M	L	A	M	J	M
X	R	Q	S	R	D	L	Z	A	Z	H	P	R	R
C	K	A	R	D	X	V	T	I	I	F	N	D	T
R	H	O	W	B	T	N	H	L	S	G	P	Z	A
L	M	Y	S	O	V	M	Y	L	N	J	O	N	U
F	A	B	J	V	H	E	M	I	J	K	H	P	T
U	A	H	U	T	J	N	E	W	M	A	N	X	U

SOLUTION ON PAGE 153

| MORRICONE | WILLIAMS | HOWARD | ZIMMER | DESPLAT |
| GIACCHINO | NEWMAN | POWELL | ELFMAN | SHORE |

Changing Landscapes of Film Distribution

```
E F N G U Z Z D Z X G D L S R X O D I
S W F R S S N A H J G N I W O D N I W
V W U V J L I O R A I J Y J N L V G L
B I A B E I M L I X O W L Y L Q T I R
G V F W M U P N F T F R A E J B B T Q
R N G C R N G W F Q P D C Y K C C A L
G C I Q P G B O G D S I I D Z C E L H
J T S M G W K D G G F J R C X I I R Y
Q A D Q A J R G N F P K T C N O N E G
C C E I S E E K O Y G R A O S B A L A
S N K K N L R X O N G R E S M B E E B
M W N T G N O T W N D D H M N Q U A V
E P A G S B X O S H J E T B I G L S P
L L M Z L F L Q V Y B K M P U E R E A
I G T Y S D S Y A K A L Z A G G R D P
L M F W U P O R U G Z Y F K N X P E P
M I E N J A F X Z W Y L K X V D M S J
A Q J Y K O Q O R J F G D K R Y W Z H
O B O T W C V Z T V A Y K Z C Z S W V
```

SOLUTION ON PAGE 154

DIGITALRELEASE   **WINDOWING**   **STREAMING**   **PREMIERE**   **ONDEMAND**
SUBSCRIPTION   **DOWNLOAD**   **BOXOFFICE**   **RENTAL**   **THEATRICAL**

Sean Penn, in a still from "Milk," Dir. by Gus Van Sant (2009)

Milk. Inspiration & Activism

Cinema has always had the ability to influence society, and "Milk," directed by Gus Van Sant in 2008, is an excellent example of how a film can capture the essence of a social movement and the impact of a charismatic leader. The film tells the story of Harvey Milk, the first openly gay politician elected to public office in California, and his fight for LGBTQ+ equality and rights in the 1970s.

Sean Penn, known for his deep immersion in his characters, delivered one of his most powerful performances as Harvey Milk. His ability to capture Milk's passion, humor, and vulnerability earned him the Oscar for Best Actor in 2008. Penn's commitment to the role and his physical and emotional transformation provided a window into the soul of a man who sought not just to change laws but also hearts and minds.

The screenplay by Dustin Lance Black, also an Oscar winner, was praised for its authenticity and delicate handling of Milk's personal and political life. The film's narrative managed to balance the intimate aspects of Milk's life with his broad influence on the civil rights movement. Black, who wrote the script with a sense of urgency and purpose, contributed to creating a poignant tale that resonates long after the film ends.

Set in San Francisco, the film captures not only the challenges and triumphs of the fight for LGBTQ+ rights but also paints an evocative portrait of the era. Van Sant's direction provides a sincere and direct look at activism, politics, and tragedy, while the cinematography and production design vividly recreate the era's atmosphere.

"Milk" was not only a critical and commercial success but also a catalyst in the conversation about LGBTQ+ equality. The 8 Oscar nominations the film received attest to its quality and relevance. The performances, combined with the direction and script, created a cinematic work that is both a tribute and a call to action, highlighting the importance of visionary leaders and resilience in the face of adversity.

The film's legacy transcends its recognition at the Academy Awards. It has become an educational cornerstone and an inspiration for activists and filmmakers alike, demonstrating that cinema can be a powerful tool for social change. Through the story of Harvey Milk, the film invites reflection on the ongoing struggle for human rights and the importance of visibility and representation. "Milk's" contribution to cinematic culture and its impact on social discourse underline the unbreakable power of socially engaged cinema in the history of the industry.

Social Impact Films

```
K A A A H F Z U K C X D Z P S C F S
L J G X S N X Y A M N I W K H M Y X
U X E O A O Q C A X W Y P M Q E S V
U A M O R U C S Z P S S Z O K J J N
A H B D C R M I C R F E Z Q R P O L
H T A Q S Z K I A H A C R H Z U W H
R U B F Z R F H L L P K B B W N E C
N U E R X F P M Q K N N M P H U R V
J E L C A J Q O Z T E E F J F H S S
B X B R B P C O X A H Z T W F T L G
J F T N F G Q N O Y C R J W M M A S
G Q V P V O K L V L C T U N O K Y M
I S S P O T L I G H T Q I D L R T V
N B J E P M U G O C W O M M I S K L
W D S U L A O H Q V H A L A W R D C
G F D A P M D T Z O B K N T H E F E
I Z P K G H A V F G K A U L H L R M
E Y O V T L T L V J V M D L F M D G
```

SOLUTION ON PAGE 154

SOCIALNETWORK **SPOTLIGHT** **TRAFFIC** **CRASH** **ROMA**
MOONLIGHT **SYRIANA** **SELMA** **MILK** **BABEL**

Robert Downey Jr. in a still from 'Iron Man' Dir. by Jon Favreau (2008)

Superhero Tsunami

The last two decades have witnessed a tsunami in superhero movies, a visual and narrative saga that has reshaped the film industry. From Marvel's rise with "Iron Man" (2008), where Robert Downey Jr.'s brilliant portrayal of Tony Stark not only redefined the superhero figure in cinema but also laid the first stone of what would be a monumental cinematic building, to the apocalyptic "Avengers: Endgame" in 2019, we have seen how CGI technology has not only revolutionized the visual experience but also enhanced the narrative, allowing each feat of our heroes to transcend the imaginable.

The resurgence of Batman in "The Dark Knight" by the great Christopher Nolan and the glorious appearance of "Wonder Woman" illustrate how DC has contributed to the modern mythological tapestry with its own dark and nuanced approach. Each of these films has been a reflection of our aspirations and fears, offering both an escape and a mirror to society.

The arrival of "Deadpool" was a revolution and a declaration of intent towards modernity and irreverence. "Deadpool" reinvented what it means to be a superhero (and technically, Deadpool is an antihero, given his unconventional style and ambiguous morality) and although Deadpool is a creation of Fabian Nicieza and Rob Liefeld for Marvel Comics, first appearing in "New Mutants" #98 in 1990, Reynolds was key in bringing the character to the big screen. Reynolds not only played Deadpool but also immersed himself in the production, helping to shape the creative direction of the films. The character's integration into the Marvel Cinematic Universe was confirmed after Disney's acquisition of 21st Century Fox, and fans eagerly await how Reynolds and the creative team will take the antihero to the next stage in the third part of the saga alongside iconic characters like Wolverine, evidently played by Hugh Jackman, which will be titled "Deadpool & Wolverine" (2024).

Behind every great Marvel movie was the complicit smile of Stan Lee, the dream architect whose cameos were as eagerly awaited as the movie itself. His legacy lives on in every film and every new iteration of his timeless creations.

As the industry advances, it faces the challenge of excess and genre fatigue, but the key is in innovation and the exploration of new themes and genres. Diversification and the ability to adapt to the times will maintain the vitality of superhero cinema. The question is no longer whether the genre can sustain itself, but how it will continue to evolve and surprise an increasingly informed and demanding global audience. Producers face the challenge of maintaining quality and innovation while meeting the demand for new content. The evolution of the genre requires a strategic approach to keep it fresh and captivating.

With technological advances and AI, each superhero and each story offers a vast field for limitless creativity. The future of superhero movies promises to be as bright and exciting as the plots that have captured our attention so far, although it will not be easy. The possibilities are as infinite as the universes inhabited by our heroes, but the public may be somewhat saturated. The challenge for creators is to continue pushing us to the limits of our imagination and beyond, in every sequence, in every conflict, and in every victory.

Evolution of Superhero Movies

P	L	L	Q	Y	A	W	C	X	O	Y	J	B	O	S	A
E	R	X	Z	V	Z	G	P	D	I	M	G	L	V	Y	F
N	P	E	U	Y	X	U	T	S	Q	F	K	Y	A	S	K
J	E	X	R	Y	V	A	F	Z	K	Y	U	M	W	V	O
B	R	M	Y	S	B	R	S	X	G	C	E	N	X	N	G
E	V	J	X	B	P	D	X	X	R	I	D	A	E	O	N
J	P	Z	U	K	P	I	S	S	F	P	L	M	L	R	E
R	Z	Z	O	W	G	A	D	U	N	E	O	O	Y	U	W
E	F	W	I	U	Z	N	E	E	V	S	O	W	A	N	T
O	A	Q	E	N	A	S	L	R	R	R	P	R	Y	N	N
G	J	C	H	K	A	I	A	E	O	M	D	E	Y	C	A
K	X	L	B	F	W	M	G	H	V	U	A	D	S	K	T
I	R	O	N	M	A	N	T	R	K	L	E	N	Y	Y	K
H	L	V	G	E	E	W	U	A	C	Y	D	O	R	J	Z
D	R	X	I	V	Z	S	K	O	B	H	O	W	V	S	O
I	Y	I	A	U	N	H	L	V	Y	U	Y	X	E	E	X

SOLUTION ON PAGE 154

| WONDERWOMAN | AVENGERS | SPIDERMAN | XMEN | BATMAN |
| GUARDIANS | IRONMAN | DEADPOOL | THOR | MARVEL |

The Impact of the Digital Age on the Industry

Social media has wielded a transformative influence on the 21st-century film industry, redefining how movies are promoted, discussed, and ultimately experienced. This shift has been multifaceted, impacting everything from production to the final reception by the audience.

Movie marketing campaigns have evolved exponentially with social media. These platforms allow for direct and personalized interaction with viewers, providing a channel to launch trailers, behind-the-scenes content, exclusive interviews, and interactive promotional material. Viral strategies and hashtags have become crucial tools for generating anticipation and discussion around releases.

This interactive revolution has democratized film criticism, allowing any viewer to share their opinion and critique instantly. This immediate feedback can influence the public perception of a movie well before traditional reviews are available, and in some cases, can impact a film's commercial success.

Social media platforms have opened new avenues for independent filmmakers, allowing them to promote their projects directly to a potential audience, generate interest, and in some cases, raise funds through crowdfunding campaigns. This has somewhat democratized film production, enabling smaller projects and diverse voices to find their audience.

They have also facilitated the emergence and spread of social movements within the industry, such as #MeToo and #OscarsSoWhite, sparking important discussions about equality, diversity, and inclusion in cinema. These movements have influenced casting decisions, movie themes, and overall industry practices.

The way we consume movies has also changed. Recommendations and critiques shared on social media influence viewers' decisions about which movies to watch. Moreover, a movie's success on social media can lead streaming platforms to acquire it, thus altering traditional distribution routes.

The impact of social media has added an extra dimension to 21st-century cinema, connecting creators more closely with their audience and vice versa, and influencing almost all aspects of the film industry. The ability to adapt to this new digital reality is now an essential component for success in the contemporary industry.

Social Media & Cinema

E	H	J	W	H	E	M	I	M	M	N	J	Z	M	L
M	I	V	F	I	F	W	F	W	V	V	N	Q	W	H
U	A	D	P	H	K	E	B	X	Q	G	L	X	P	T
E	M	E	M	G	E	J	X	O	J	J	Z	I	V	W
V	R	G	R	C	H	N	R	X	F	L	J	P	U	O
L	S	A	T	T	A	R	T	D	V	N	R	H	V	G
A	L	F	L	I	S	B	Z	A	A	X	O	R	V	Z
R	B	S	R	Z	H	Z	V	I	V	O	J	H	U	F
I	H	U	S	M	T	W	G	C	U	F	F	P	L	G
V	H	I	H	A	A	O	W	Z	Y	S	A	K	Q	X
C	K	Y	A	B	G	O	L	G	N	U	R	O	M	F
W	X	E	R	Y	L	P	H	L	O	Q	C	X	L	L
J	D	I	E	L	L	O	I	Y	E	P	N	K	E	G
J	M	G	O	L	V	K	G	T	R	W	M	K	R	X
I	N	F	L	U	E	N	C	E	R	D	L	E	Y	L

SOLUTION ON PAGE 154

| INFLUENCER | FOLLOW | VIRAL | SHARE | MEME |
| HASHTAG | STREAM | BLOG | VLOG | LIKE |

Joaquin Phoenix in one of the most impactful frames of "Joker" by Todd Philips (2019)

The JOKER of Joaquin Phoenix

"Joker", directed by Todd Phillips in 2019 and featuring Joaquin Phoenix, marked a milestone in modern cinema, redefining the comic book movie genre with its focus on intense character study and deeply psychological narrative. Set in Gotham City in 1981, the film presents an alternative origin story for the iconic DC Comics villain. Arthur Fleck, a failed comedian whose descent into madness and nihilism sparks a violent revolution against the elite in a decaying city.

The creative process behind Joker was unique from the start. Joaquin Phoenix, known for his meticulous role selection and commitment to each character, was drawn to the idea of a low-budget film centered on a comic book villain. Phillips and Silver's vision, inspired by 1970s character films and Martin Scorsese's work, provided fertile ground for this complex narrative. The main filming, primarily conducted in and around New York, captured the essence of a Gotham reflecting the social and economic turmoil of the time.

Joker's premiere at the 76th Venice International Film Festival, where it won the prestigious Golden Lion, was just the beginning of its critical and commercial success. The film became a cultural phenomenon, sparking debates on topics such as mental health, social alienation, and the ethical implications of its portrayal of violence.

The film's impact extended to the awards season, particularly at the 2020 Oscars. Joaquin Phoenix received the Best Actor Oscar for his unforgettable portrayal of Arthur Fleck, elevating his career to new heights and solidifying his status as one of the most versatile and committed actors of his generation. Hildur Guðnadóttir won the Best Original Score award, marking a historic moment as one of the few women to win in this category and the first to do so solo in over two decades.

Phoenix's performance was at the heart of Joker's acclaim. His transformation into Arthur Fleck was both a physical and emotional feat, capturing the tragic humanity and unsettling unraveling of the character.

Joker received 11 Oscar nominations, including Best Picture, and stood out as the most nominated comic book-inspired film in the history of these awards, even surpassing The Dark Knight (2008). This recognition underscores the film's ability to transcend its genre and resonate deeply with both audiences and critics.

Despite the controversies and discussions surrounding its release, Joker proved to be a cinematic work that transcends entertainment to become a mirror of the complexities and darkness of contemporary society. The film not only left an indelible mark on the superhero genre but also redefined what a comic book movie can be, merging the art of cinema with deep social and psychological commentary. Joker's acclaim at the Oscars and its box office success are testimonies to its resonance with the public and critics alike, ensuring its place as one of the most significant and impactful films of recent times.

"Joker" is more than a comic book movie; it's a heart-wrenching character study that challenges the audience to reflect on the fractures in our society and what drives an individual to the edge. Phoenix's performance, Phillips's direction, and the bold narrative ensure that Joker endures as a contemporary classic, remembered not only for its controversy but for its ability to capture the complexity of the human spirit and a sick and decaying society.

Iconic Film Characters of the 21st Century

```
C C C D Q F X C U E W P A B H O
W T W O L V E R I N E M O H Y G
Z W Y X Q H W D H Y D K G Y N G
T Y W O T B Y K I R H O J E H H
Y V W O D I W K C A L B Z B U K
D M Y S R E K U X L X Z V V L R
M R O S P R D E U U K Y E H K L
H J R I M O A M U V L O O U X M
L F U N A D K P H X K E R H S L
C Q X T O E E T S M N B F G J Y
I S D A W L P R E K O J T Q Q M
W W B K M B U H Z W C Y N R Y P
U R B B M M K I J P E A S I J P
J P H N X U W J G E M I J E X K
G Y M F H D V K D P B O V D A A
M K X N K P F J R U U J F A F A
```

SOLUTION ON PAGE 155

DUMBLERDORE   **BLACKWIDOW**   **GOLLUM**   **HULK**   **SHREK**
JACKSPARROW   **WOLVERINE**   **KATNISS**   **NEO**   **JOKER**

Christopher Nolan directing Cillian Murphy in a sequence from "Oppenheimer" (2023)

Christopher Nolan

Christopher Nolan is one of the most distinguished and respected directors of his generation. Born on July 30, 1970, in London, Nolan began making films in his youth before studying English literature at the University of London. His first feature film, "Following" (2000), established his style of nonlinear storytelling and complex themes.

He has solidified his reputation as one of the most visionary filmmakers of our era. His work spans a variety of genres, including the psychological thriller with "Memento" (2001), the epic space drama in "Interstellar" (2014), and the meticulous character study in "The Prestige" (2006). Nolan stands out for his preference for complex narratives and non-linear script structures, his ability to combine profound themes with great spectacle, and his commitment to practical filming and minimal use of CGI. The "The Dark Knight" trilogy (2008) is particularly emblematic, as it not only revitalized the superhero genre and "Batman" himself but also posed philosophical questions about justice and chaos.

Nolan's career is also notable for his emphasis on the cinema experience. He is a staunch advocate for the use of film format and IMAX presentations and has constantly pushed the boundaries of what is possible in terms of cinematic viewing. His dedication to authenticity and his ability to inject humanity and complexity into his stories have profoundly influenced the industry.

His latest film, "Oppenheimer" (2023), starring Cillian Murphy and featuring a supporting cast that includes Robert Downey Jr. and Emily Blunt, is a dramatic and meticulously researched exploration of the figure of J. Robert Oppenheimer, known as the "father of the atomic bomb." The film examines the development of the Manhattan Project during World War II and the moral implications of this powerful new technology. Through Nolan's lens, Oppenheimer's complex personality is examined, a man whose extraordinary talents and ambitions confronted him with deeply disturbing ethical dilemmas.

With "Oppenheimer," Nolan has not only created an impactful biographical portrait but has also continued his exploration of themes of time, memory, and human nature. The use of large-format film formats such as IMAX and the renunciation of computer-generated effects in favor of practical effects and in-camera recordings are a testament to his unique approach to filmmaking. The immersive sound design and Ludwig Göransson's score deepen the viewer's emotional experience, creating a work that is not only visually and auditorily impressive but also intellectually stimulating.

The film has not only been critically acclaimed but has also received notable recognition at the latest Oscars, winning seven statuettes including Best Picture, Best Actor, and Best Director. Downey Jr.'s recognition with the Oscar for Best Supporting Actor underscores Nolan's ability to extract powerful and memorable performances from his cast.

The story of Oppenheimer and his internal struggle captures the essence of human dilemmas in the face of scientific advancement. The film invites viewers to contemplate the price of innovation and the inherent responsibility of those who push the boundaries of human knowledge. Nolan presents Oppenheimer not as one-dimensional hero or villain but as a complex man who was central in one of the most critical moments in modern history.

Ultimately, "Oppenheimer" is yet another example of how Nolan continues to challenge and enrich modern cinema, combining deep storytelling with impressive cinematographic achievements. His passion for telling meaningful stories, his technical mastery, and his ability to engage the audience in fundamental issues ensure that his place in film history is more than consolidated.

Revolutionary Directors of the 2000s

I	E	T	G	H	C	O	E	N	J	Q	H	S	N	B
P	O	B	H	V	R	D	Z	N	I	Z	S	Z	T	N
D	R	F	G	R	E	B	L	E	I	P	S	R	T	K
M	O	R	R	O	B	S	F	A	X	Q	E	S	S	T
X	T	U	E	X	S	H	K	R	C	X	M	R	D	Z
Q	L	A	B	G	U	D	W	Q	F	U	M	B	O	J
L	E	N	R	J	C	V	J	I	Q	B	D	Z	P	E
U	D	D	E	A	A	N	N	N	V	A	P	N	I	B
L	G	E	D	N	N	C	R	S	O	B	Z	O	V	Y
F	G	R	O	J	H	T	K	M	G	L	Z	T	A	O
H	V	S	S	E	S	Z	I	S	Y	Q	A	L	J	O
Z	C	O	R	E	M	S	O	N	O	A	W	N	T	H
C	F	N	Q	P	R	J	B	T	O	N	T	V	E	N
K	N	Y	Y	U	M	C	E	Q	J	Q	G	O	H	Z
U	V	Y	K	L	O	E	H	I	O	B	O	F	V	V

SOLUTION ON PAGE 155

SODERBERGH   ANDERSON   DELTORO   NOLAN   FINCHER
TARANTINO   SPIELBERG   JACKSON   COEN   LYNCH

SOLUTIONS

Early Cinema Days
1895 - 1940

P.9

Silent Film Stars
1900 - 1920

P.11

Silent Film Innovations

P.12

Silent Film Pionners

P.13

Transition to Sound
1927

R	U	K	D	M	B	I	Z	H	K	R	H	B	I	V
U	S	E	I	M	I	U	T	Y	E	R	O	C	S	N
G	K	V	A	Z	Q	C	W	M	N	V	O	F	R	T
U	D	N	L	O	O	P	R	P	O	K	I	L	A	U
Q	Z	O	O	K	Z	R	I	O	H	E	K	A	A	K
T	H	R	G	F	M	V	V	K	P	K	L	M	G	F
H	E	C	U	R	V	R	Q	T	A	H	P	W	P	G
W	Y	W	E	M	X	E	V	W	T	L	O	L	U	H
H	M	T	F	K	I	N	F	E	I	I	J	N	A	A
B	X	Z	U	O	Y	T	M	F	V	G	M	J	E	P
P	P	Z	U	Q	L	Q	I	A	E	I	X	D	V	G
K	T	A	L	K	I	E	S	Y	N	C	M	T	L	G
E	T	J	S	E	R	I	Y	Y	K	K	T	C	G	Y
U	M	Y	V	S	U	L	X	L	K	K	D	S	Q	V
J	S	M	Z	Q	X	G	U	B	P	K	S	O	A	J

P.15

Pioneering Women in Early Cinema

V	Q	I	S	W	U	X	Z	P	F	S	S	D
V	Z	Y	Q	F	S	D	W	G	P	Z	P	N
J	X	G	B	R	Y	W	F	F	I	I	A	R
X	I	E	Y	U	O	I	O	L	C	S	G	I
Y	C	U	Y	U	W	B	B	K	B	T	H	D
Z	O	E	I	S	R	D	F	Q	S	A	S	E
W	O	L	R	A	H	O	L	E	A	N	M	S
S	M	Q	G	S	R	E	W	B	O	W	B	N
E	P	Q	B	D	S	Y	A	R	W	Y	A	M
G	V	L	R	D	I	E	T	R	I	C	H	S
D	Z	B	N	W	J	X	O	R	E	K	C	O
T	B	I	H	T	J	V	E	Z	R	R	G	Y
Z	Q	E	P	F	S	Q	D	X	H	Z	P	G

P.17

1930s Adventure & Action

I	U	K	R	W	H	G	N	Z	E	C	B	H	J	J	N	G
W	E	S	T	E	R	N	D	P	U	D	O	X	D	P	X	G
I	G	S	U	V	L	T	D	S	G	G	P	Z	P	G	L	F
D	L	N	O	U	B	K	T	J	O	E	V	G	D	B	V	M
Y	F	Z	O	R	R	O	C	U	R	B	P	O	Y	A	T	Q
B	A	C	V	K	H	E	G	U	E	I	V	B	J	R	I	X
A	I	U	U	A	F	C	T	P	B	O	Y	N	U	I	E	V
T	R	M	O	L	K	N	Z	S	R	H	Z	H	O	R	M	H
P	B	S	Y	T	E	X	Y	L	G	I	S	Z	H	S	V	T
J	A	N	T	V	T	L	D	O	N	N	W	A	A	S	P	N
W	N	Y	D	A	A	G	O	G	Q	I	A	Y	W	W	F	C
C	K	A	B	B	R	C	N	J	V	D	I	G	C	S	D	A
R	S	J	U	Q	I	Z	B	R	S	L	R	O	G	E	E	E
I	S	O	Q	E	P	B	A	G	U	R	E	S	W	F	C	F
Y	S	U	V	L	X	V	Q	N	T	E	O	F	E	E	C	E
C	S	Z	D	P	I	J	N	B	N	A	J	M	F	K	H	K
X	I	D	D	D	T	W	F	P	E	L	Q	C	K	U	W	O

P.19

1930s Golden Age Begins

N	J	U	S	Y	A	O	Z	D	Y	N	B	W	G
K	Q	T	S	C	R	Y	N	R	T	T	L	U	X
G	Z	R	N	M	O	O	R	A	I	X	F	B	B
Q	M	G	C	U	W	M	M	M	E	O	W	U	O
S	A	V	X	S	O	B	E	A	J	F	N	L	P
W	K	X	X	I	Y	M	V	D	N	N	C	I	M
F	B	D	O	C	L	M	A	V	I	C	X	V	Q
Y	M	J	K	A	L	J	M	R	V	A	E	K	Y
V	I	V	F	L	J	T	E	K	A	A	C	T	V
S	E	L	T	J	W	N	T	Y	J	P	A	Q	I
S	X	A	P	X	R	S	R	A	D	I	O	X	Y
M	M	L	H	A	L	R	O	A	R	B	N	N	U
Q	E	T	W	M	Z	V	P	G	T	I	P	B	K
Y	Z	C	F	Z	E	F	H	Y	C	U	V	N	K

P.21

1930s Genres

F	T	N	R	U	K	U	U	Z	Y	V	G	Y	T	U
E	U	V	E	R	S	Z	Z	L	W	B	G	Y	E	G
P	D	C	V	U	Q	C	G	K	C	V	S	J	C	G
V	M	H	I	S	T	O	R	I	C	A	L	U	N	Q
H	X	Q	T	P	D	C	Y	E	T	L	O	A	O	A
W	B	M	C	R	O	B	H	N	W	R	D	Q	M	S
F	K	W	E	D	O	I	A	B	I	B	F	R	O	K
Q	T	K	T	L	H	F	B	V	P	R	A	Y	R	S
Y	U	H	E	S	O	X	J	W	F	A	A	L	V	C
M	U	T	D	K	H	D	P	M	H	W	L	W	L	K
L	K	O	K	Y	V	P	R	A	F	F	I	G	T	M
J	R	O	R	R	O	H	G	A	N	G	S	T	E	R
S	C	C	Q	R	H	G	C	N	M	R	Q	K	Z	T
S	V	V	P	M	J	S	M	X	Y	A	E	P	U	E
N	D	X	L	H	F	E	O	W	T	I	O	G	X	D

P.22

1930s Actresses

E	K	Q	K	H	E	P	B	U	R	N	V	L
O	S	G	I	M	G	T	G	S	S	J	G	F
S	G	R	N	K	R	I	G	U	Z	I	J	N
T	I	C	E	O	C	V	E	X	A	E	Q	X
J	B	V	R	G	Q	Y	P	L	F	H	O	U
K	A	E	A	A	O	D	W	O	G	C	Z	W
U	Z	Y	K	D	W	R	Z	N	D	I	C	F
E	L	I	B	H	F	F	H	N	A	R	W	E
O	R	D	R	A	B	M	O	L	T	T	K	S
Q	C	H	C	R	P	B	V	R	D	E	S	T
F	W	B	Y	L	K	R	Q	A	D	I	F	S
D	B	U	Y	O	L	A	S	N	W	D	T	P
J	M	K	P	W	O	R	N	V	R	M	Z	G

P.24

1930s Actors

D	G	G	R	K	F	M	S	D	T	D	X
Z	A	A	A	P	I	F	C	Y	R	F	B
E	B	S	B	F	F	O	L	R	A	K	G
R	L	T	C	P	N	O	Y	H	W	C	D
F	E	A	D	N	O	F	E	A	E	H	B
Y	T	I	G	B	C	H	N	V	T	W	R
I	L	R	V	X	U	T	G	R	S	F	G
D	C	E	B	I	S	B	A	Y	H	L	M
Z	Z	A	A	O	L	G	C	W	W	S	S
L	Q	R	E	P	O	O	C	C	O	J	N
D	B	C	O	B	L	T	L	N	A	K	Z
V	P	C	K	V	Y	G	R	A	N	T	T

P.26

1930s Film Innovations

Y	I	A	I	H	X	O	T	H	C	P	J	Q	F	Z	M
D	Q	Y	T	H	P	R	D	Q	O	R	E	W	C	Q	K
X	V	I	D	E	Q	I	S	Z	L	O	M	V	C	S	L
N	M	Q	N	F	C	M	H	I	D	T	K	J	H	O	N
N	P	H	U	V	Z	H	A	S	A	U	R	X	R	U	K
J	E	S	U	G	G	R	N	C	R	W	D	G	O	N	C
E	V	W	R	Q	I	P	Q	I	H	O	D	I	M	D	H
F	P	G	S	U	B	B	P	I	C	X	S	A	A	T	B
G	E	G	P	R	R	R	V	U	W	O	E	N	K	R	Z
S	J	F	S	L	E	I	M	G	C	F	L	V	E	A	X
U	L	E	Y	C	G	E	H	J	I	L	V	O	Y	C	T
K	Q	F	O	S	N	L	L	Q	X	O	C	Z	R	K	C
D	E	D	I	T	I	N	G	C	K	D	O	P	V	B	A
Y	E	S	A	N	I	M	A	T	I	O	N	K	Q	R	C
C	H	R	D	C	H	V	S	P	M	D	T	Z	O	C	S
M	Y	F	S	M	Y	S	D	F	L	Y	T	L	C	N	O

P.27

War-Time Cinema

P.29

International Cinema of the Era

P.30

Key Films of the Golden Age

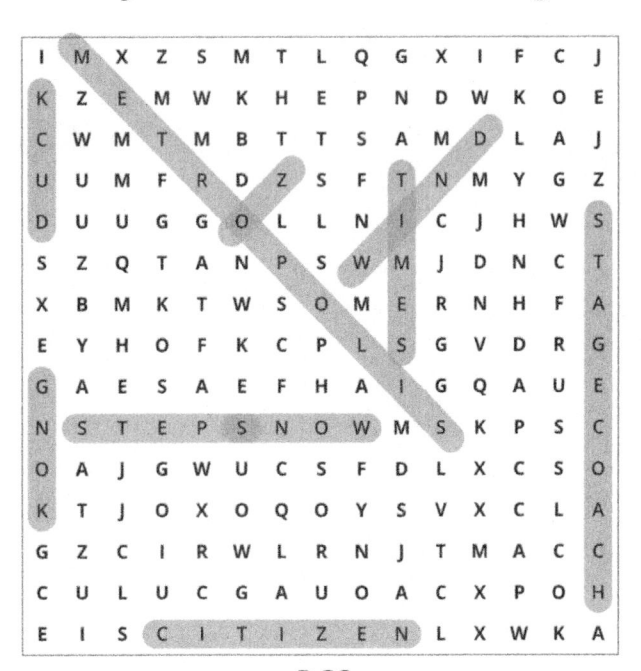

P.32

Industry Changes

P.34

Early Animation & Cartoons

P.36

Great Film Directors of the 1930s

P.38

Iconic 1930s Film Characters

P.39

Breakthroughs in Film Sound & Music

P.41

The Impact of the Great Depression on Cinema

P.43

Major Film Studios of the Golden Age

P.44

Notable Film Critics & Theorists

P.46

Advances in Film Technology

P.47

Landmark Films of the Era

(word search puzzle, P.48)

Hollywood during World War II

(word search puzzle, P.51)

Post-War Cinema

(word search puzzle, P.52)

Golden Age Film Stars

(word search puzzle, P.54)

1950s and 1960s Directors

P.56

Iconic Films of the 1950s

P.58

Rise of Television

P.59

New Wave Movements

P.60

Sci-Fi and Fantasy of the 1960s

P.61

Music & Concert Films

P.63

Social Revolution in Cinema

P.65

Cinema in the Cold War

P.66

Major Film Genres of the 1970s & 1980s

P.68

Blockbuster Era Begins

P.70

New Hollywood Directors

P.72

Iconic Actors & Actresses of the 70s & 80s

P.74

146

Influential International Cinema

P.76

1980s Teen & Family Films

P.78

Advances in Film Technology

P.80

Cult Films & Movements

P.82

Documentary & Realism

(word search grid, P.83)

Rise of Action Heroes & Superheroes

(word search grid, P.85)

Landmark Science Fiction Films

(word search grid, P.87)

Comedy Icons of the 70s & 80s

(word search grid, P.89)

Influential Female Directors

P.91

Breakthrough in Animation & Special Effects

P.93

Cinema in the 1990s

P.96

Influential Films of the 1990s

P.98

Rise of Animation Studios

P.100

Major Film Genres of the 90s & 2000s

P.101

2000s New Wave & Indie Directors

P.103

Global Cinema in the New Millennium

P.105

Influential 2000s Films

(P.107)

Modern Animation & CGI Advances

(P.108)

Documentary Films & Realism

(P.111)

Rise of Streaming Services

(P.112)

21st Century Film Technology

P.113

New Genres & Trends

P.114

Influential Women in Modern Cinema

P.116

Modern Science Fiction & Fantasy

P.117

Independent Cinema Evolution

R	Q	B	S	A	W	Y	I	K	W	E	A	Q	K
E	X	R	D	M	K	S	O	J	B	B	A	F	M
L	E	X	N	O	E	N	H	D	E	I	D	N	I
E	H	S	J	R	A	W	E	A	I	Q	W	A	R
V	F	B	U	T	N	K	T	I	K	N	J	R	A
T	C	A	L	N	Q	D	A	L	W	Q	U	T	M
I	L	F	Q	U	D	T	G	Z	E	S	O	I	A
Q	G	H	I	J	M	A	S	W	U	K	S	S	X
E	T	A	I	J	S	H	N	C	B	D	E	A	J
N	C	X	N	D	U	V	O	C	A	K	F	N	Q
P	I	E	M	K	T	F	I	U	E	D	D	S	Z
D	I	F	W	N	H	U	L	T	S	M	F	E	I
P	F	Z	W	K	H	U	Y	K	E	E	P	D	A
V	A	M	A	G	N	O	L	I	A	D	R	H	P

P.119

Global Box Office Hits

T	R	A	N	S	F	O	R	M	E	R	S	R	Y	P	I	Q
A	Q	F	V	G	T	M	N	J	J	X	K	L	J	R	J	M
F	F	Q	M	A	A	O	E	E	M	B	L	K	D	B	I	G
F	U	G	X	L	T	K	Z	J	Z	L	L	W	M	C	S	S
G	T	Q	L	I	L	A	O	M	M	Z	Z	R	T	Z	B	I
S	M	C	Z	D	Y	A	R	W	P	M	G	A	W	O	T	K
N	D	I	P	I	P	N	F	D	K	T	D	W	B	G	I	T
P	F	A	N	O	Z	D	Y	Y	I	Z	O	N	I	V	L	D
X	C	E	B	I	M	N	X	T	K	E	K	E	N	O	Y	Q
R	Q	A	Z	V	O	I	A	I	H	S	K	G	C	Q	R	L
P	A	N	N	U	G	N	E	N	D	G	A	M	E	V	D	I
Y	G	P	V	E	I	X	S	J	O	Q	I	R	P	R	L	U
E	J	U	L	C	M	W	M	K	U	O	V	L	T	J	V	W
Z	N	R	J	Q	R	Y	L	A	W	K	T	A	I	A	X	V
R	N	Z	B	T	R	Z	M	K	D	O	D	X	O	W	I	X
G	T	S	I	K	C	A	G	U	V	F	K	M	N	M	T	F
M	G	Y	D	Q	N	X	L	I	X	F	W	K	U	M	U	C

P.121

Trends in 21st Century Storytelling

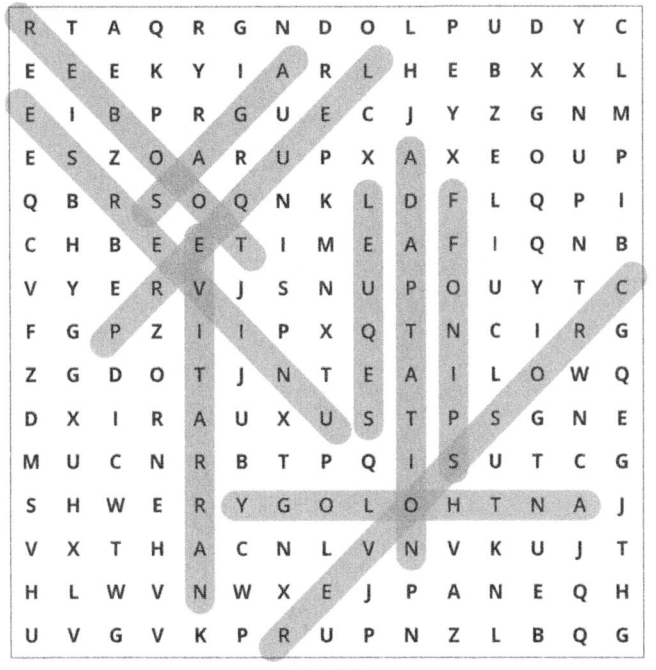

R	T	A	Q	R	G	N	D	O	L	P	U	D	Y	C
E	E	E	K	Y	I	A	R	L	H	E	B	X	X	L
E	I	B	P	R	G	U	E	C	J	Y	Z	G	N	M
E	S	Z	O	A	R	U	P	X	A	X	E	O	U	P
Q	B	R	S	O	Q	N	K	L	D	F	L	Q	P	I
C	H	B	E	E	T	I	M	E	A	F	I	Q	N	B
V	Y	E	R	V	J	S	N	U	P	O	U	Y	T	C
F	G	P	Z	I	I	P	X	Q	T	N	C	I	R	G
Z	G	D	O	T	J	N	T	E	A	I	L	O	W	Q
D	X	I	R	A	U	X	U	S	T	P	S	G	N	E
M	U	C	N	R	B	T	P	Q	I	S	U	T	C	G
S	H	W	E	R	Y	G	O	L	O	H	T	N	A	J
V	X	T	H	A	C	N	L	V	N	V	K	U	J	T
H	L	W	V	N	W	X	E	J	P	A	N	E	Q	H
U	V	G	V	K	P	R	U	P	N	Z	L	B	Q	G

P.122

Modern Film Soundtracks & Scores

D	R	T	D	L	M	H	N	F	U	W	L	A	A
W	H	P	P	L	C	G	O	H	I	V	K	N	E
Q	P	O	Q	G	Q	M	D	Z	N	V	W	P	U
T	N	W	N	Z	L	Z	V	A	E	G	H	J	D
A	V	E	E	I	M	J	M	N	I	C	Y	E	C
B	V	L	R	M	H	F	O	T	V	I	S	L	X
S	E	L	O	M	L	C	J	S	E	P	F	O	A
D	P	J	H	E	I	X	C	M	L	A	M	J	M
X	R	Q	S	R	D	L	Z	A	Z	H	P	R	R
C	K	A	R	D	X	V	T	I	I	F	N	D	T
R	H	O	W	B	T	N	H	L	S	G	P	Z	A
L	M	Y	S	O	V	M	Y	L	N	J	O	N	U
F	A	B	J	V	H	E	M	I	J	K	H	P	T
U	A	H	U	T	J	N	E	W	M	A	N	X	U

P.124

Changing Landscapes of Film Distribution

P.125

Social Impact Films

P.127

Evolution of Superhero Movies

P.129

Social Media & Cinema

P.131

Iconic Film Characters of the 21st Century

C	C	C	D	Q	F	X	C	U	E	W	P	A	B	H	O
W	T	W	O	L	V	E	R	I	N	E	M	O	H	Y	G
Z	W	Y	X	Q	H	W	D	H	Y	D	K	G	Y	N	G
T	Y	W	O	T	B	Y	K	I	R	H	O	J	E	H	H
Y	V	W	O	D	I	W	K	C	A	L	B	Z	B	U	K
D	M	Y	S	R	E	K	U	X	L	Z	V	V	L	R	
M	R	O	S	P	R	D	E	U	U	K	Y	E	H	K	L
H	J	R	I	M	O	A	M	U	V	L	O	O	U	X	M
L	F	U	N	A	D	K	P	H	X	K	E	R	H	S	L
C	Q	X	T	O	E	E	T	S	M	N	B	F	G	J	Y
I	S	D	A	W	L	P	R	E	K	O	J	T	Q	Q	M
W	W	B	K	M	B	U	H	Z	W	C	Y	N	R	Y	P
U	R	B	B	M	M	K	I	J	P	E	A	S	I	J	P
J	P	H	N	X	U	W	J	G	E	M	I	J	E	X	K
G	Y	M	F	H	D	V	K	D	P	B	O	V	D	A	A
M	K	X	N	K	P	F	J	R	U	U	J	F	A	F	A

P.133

Revolutionary Directors of the 2000s

I	E	T	G	H	C	O	E	N	J	Q	H	S	N	B
P	O	B	H	V	R	D	Z	N	I	Z	S	Z	T	N
D	R	F	G	R	E	B	L	E	I	P	S	R	T	K
M	O	R	R	O	B	S	F	A	X	Q	E	S	S	T
X	T	U	E	X	S	H	K	R	C	X	M	R	D	Z
Q	L	A	B	G	U	D	W	Q	F	U	M	B	O	J
L	E	N	R	J	C	V	J	I	Q	B	D	Z	P	E
U	D	D	E	A	A	N	N	N	V	A	P	N	I	B
L	G	E	D	N	N	C	R	S	O	B	Z	O	V	Y
F	G	R	O	J	H	T	K	M	G	L	Z	T	A	O
H	V	S	S	E	S	Z	I	S	Y	Q	A	L	J	O
Z	C	O	R	E	M	S	O	N	O	A	W	N	T	H
C	F	N	Q	P	R	J	B	T	O	N	T	V	E	N
K	N	Y	Y	U	M	C	E	Q	J	Q	G	O	H	Z
U	V	Y	K	L	O	E	H	I	O	B	O	F	V	V

P.135

155

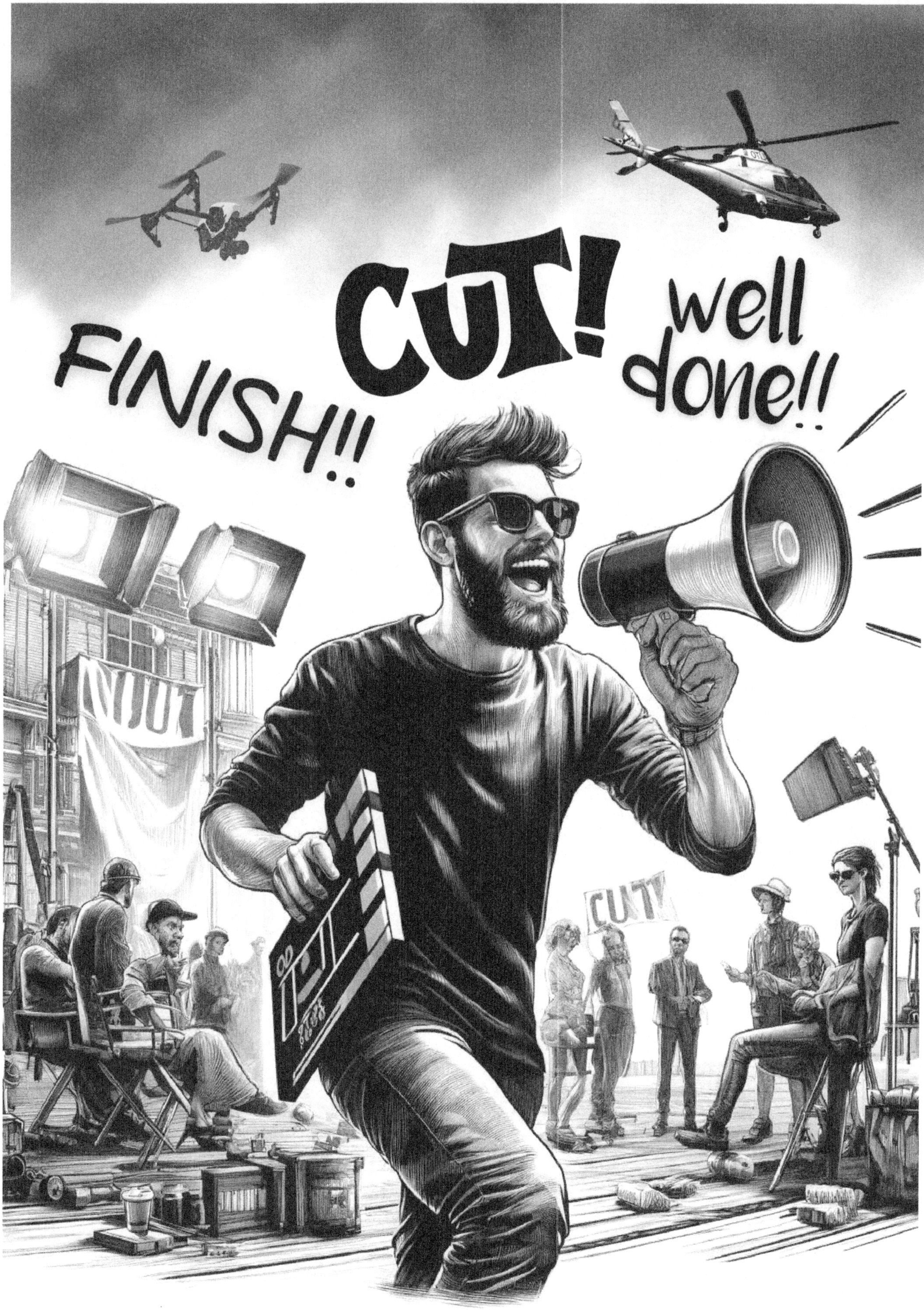
FINISH!!
CUT!
well done!!

You've made it to the end!

Congrats!

Congratulations on making it to the end!

We've taken a wonderful journey together through the history of cinema from 1895 to 2023, starting with the fathers of the Seventh Art, the Lumière brothers, moving through Chaplin, the first pioneering women in cinema, social changes and technological advancements, and arriving at Christopher Nolan, a major winner in 2023 with his film "Oppenheimer".

We know you must have missed people like Paul Newman, Sean Connery, Marlon Brando, Dustin Hoffman, Jack Nicholson, Steven Spielberg, Woody Allen, Tom Cruise, James Bond, Cary Grant, James Stewart, John Wayne, Audrey Hepburn, Lana Turner, Charlize Theron, Keanu Reeves, Marilyn Monroe, Jack Lemmon, Walter Matthau, Shirley MacLaine, Michael Caine, Sir Laurence Olivier, Charlton Heston, Bruce Willis, Sandra Bullock, Richard Gere, Julia Roberts, Andy García, Burt Lancaster, Tom Hanks, Anthony Hopkins, Spencer Tracy, Roman Polanski, Francis Ford Coppola, Natalie Wood, George Lucas, Eddie Murphy, Steve Martin, Martin Short, Gene Wilder... and a very long etcetera. But in this book, where we wanted to cover the entire history of cinema to our days, it would have been impossible to name them all.

But that doesn't mean you won't enjoy them or that we've forgotten them, FAR FROM IT!

You will find this entire list of stars in our next issue, which will be called **HOLLYWOOD UNIVERSE**, and will discuss all these stars individually, their entire filmography. Actresses, actors, directors, female directors, producers...

In the third installment of this cinematic trilogy, we will discuss the best movies in the history of cinema in our book **THE BEST MOVIES**. So, we invite you to stay tuned for our upcoming releases.

It has been a pleasure to build this book for you, movie lovers around the world, and to share it with all our enthusiasm and love for cinema through all times.

Many, many thanks for joining us on this journey. From **WORDWEABER**, we hope that for you it has been enjoyable, a moment of play, of learning by playing, and that you have discovered things you did not know and have been curious to see some of the movies you have seen in the book and are now eager to watch them, and that we have touched your nostalgia with those films you did know and have served to remind you of the moments when you saw them, who you went to the movies with, the moment of your life that impacted you some of them and what they still make you feel today about those wonderful memories. That's cinema.

We are simply here for you to enjoy playing and learning. So we will continue striving to achieve this book after book.

We would be delighted to hear your impressions of the book by reading your reviews, which will help us continue to improve.

So, we'll see you in the next book, and the journey continues!

LONG LIVE CINEMA!

"A good wine is like a good movie: it lasts a moment and leaves a taste of glory in your mouth; it's new with every sip and, as with movies, it is born and reborn in every taster."

Federico Fellini

"HISTORY OF CINEMA" is a product of WordWeaver Publishing.
Idea, design, and graphics by Julio Arrojo.
Layout and cover design by Stilo54 Communication (www.stilo54.com).
Special thanks to the Academy of Motion Picture Arts and Sciences (https://www.oscars.org/).

All rights reserved. No part of the texts, graphics, or photographs in this book may be reproduced in any form or by any means without the express permission of the author.

First edition Rome (Italy), April 13, 2024.

WORDWEABER PUBLISHING

TO BE CONTINUED....→

Printed in Great Britain
by Amazon